Fi[illegible]on in Uganda

The Process of Building a National Integrity System

Edited by

A.Ruzindana, P. Langseth & A. Gakwandi

Fountain Publishers

Fountain Publishers Ltd.
P.O. Box 488
Kampala, Uganda

First Published 1998

ISBN 9970 02 058 7

CONTENTS

Foreword By **Dr Specioza Wandira Kazibwe** v

Preface ix

Part One

BUILDING INTEGRITY: GENERAL PERSPECTIVES

1. Background to the Intergirty System 1
   Augustine Ruzindana

2. The National Integrity System in Uganda 4
   James Katorobo

3. Elements of a Successful Anti-corruption Strategy 8
   Jeremy Pope

Part Two

CORRUPTION IN UGANDA

4. Corruption in the Public Service: An Assessment 17
   Chapter 14 of the Report of the Public Service Review and Reorganisation Commission

5. Ethics, Accountability and Transparency in Uganda: An Assessment 38
   Petter Langseth and *Jeremy Pope*

Part Three

INSTITUTIONAL MECHANISMS

6. Combating corruption in Uganda 51
   Augustine Ruzindana

7. The Responsibilities of the Government, the Media and the Public in Combating Corruption 70
Damian Kato

8. The Role of the Inspector General of Government 75
Matthias B. Tumwesigye

9. Good Governance and Control of Corruption 79
James Kahoza

Part Four

LOCAL INTERGRITY SYSTEM

10. On-Going Reforms Relevant to Curbing Corruption: The Contribution of Decentralisation 91
F.X.K. Lubanga

11. Capacity Buidling with Results-Orientation and Integrity in Mind: The Experience of Uganda 97
Mohammad A.M. Kisubi

Part Five

THE ROLE OF THE ENFORECEMENT AGENCIES

12. The Director of Public Prosecutions and Crime Prevention 109
Alfred P. W. Nasaba

13. The Role of the Police in Fighting Corruption 128
John Cossy Odomel

Part Six

ROLE OF THE MEDIA

14. The State of the Media in Uganda 131
Amos Kajoba

15. The Media: A Pillar in Fighting Corruption 141
Eric Ogoso Opolot

16. Investigative Journalism: The Mutual Roles of the Media and the Civil Service in Exposing Misconduct 148
James Katorobo

Part Seven

INTERNATIONAL PARTNERS

17. Building Integrity to Fight Corruption: A PartnershipBetween Uganda, TI and EDI to Improve Service Delivery to the Public 159
Petter Langseth

CONTRIBUTORS

James Kahoza is the Auditor General, Government of Uganda.

Amos Kajoba is Editor of *The People*, a Kampala-based newspaper.

Damian Kato is Permanent Secretary to the Inspector General of Government.

James Katorobo is an International Consultant, currently with UNDP in New York.

Mohammed A.M. Kisubi is an International Consultant.

Petter Langseth works with the Governance and Anti-corruption Unit of the Economic Development Institute (EDI) of the World Bank in Washington.

Francis Lubanga is Permanent Secretary, Ministry of Local Government.

Alfred P. W. Nasaba is a former Director of Public Prosecutions.

John Cossy Odomel is the Inspector General of Police.

Eric Ogoso Opolot is a journalist with the *New Vision* newspaper.

Jeremy Pope is the Managing Director, Transparency International.

Augustine Ruzindana is Member of Parliament and Chairman of Public Accounts Committee (PAC)and former Inspector General of Government.

Matthias B. Tumwesigye works with the Inspector General of Government (IGG).

FOREWORD

By

Dr Specioza Wandira Kazibwe

Vice President of Uganda

Introduction

While no comprehensive legal definition of corruption exists in Uganda, corruption is understood to encompass the misuse of power, funds or resources by holder of public office for personal ends, gains, or self interest to the prejudice of public interest.

Corruption is deeply embedded in Uganda's culture. The political instability and economic degeneration that Uganda faced from independence to 1986 also contributed to widespread corruption in the country.

Corruption erodes the moral fiber of the society. It deprives society of resources that would have otherwise been used, for the development of the country.

In order to tackle corruption, Government will have to address both its manifestations and its root causes.

The institution framework to fight corruption

In Uganda, a number of institutions to fight corruption have been in place for a long time, but the country is still bedeviled with corruption. This has led into a deeply held perception in the general populace that the Government has almost lost the battle against corruption.

The institutions charged with the task of fighting corruption are the Presidency, the people of Uganda, the parliament, and the Judiciary. In addition there exists constitutional agencies specifically charged with this task. These are the Inspector General of Government (IGG), the Auditor General (AG) the Department of Public Prosecutions (DPP). The office of the Vice President co-ordinates these agencies as well as all anti-corruption activities and integrity building activities in the country. An Anti-Corruption Unit, was established within the Office of the Vice President, to assist the Vice President with these tasks.

The Constitution also guarantees the autonomy of the IGG, DPP and Auditor General. It provides for a Leadership Code of Conduct and punitive measures. In addition to the Constitution, there are other laws in place to combat corruption. These include the Prevention of Corruption Act, the Penal Code and its amendments and the Local Government Act.

Other measures to combat corruption have also been taken by the NRM Government. These include: The Economic Reform and Liberalization, the Civil Service Reform, Decentralization, and the improvement of remuneration of judicial officers, top civil servants and political leaders.

Constraints hampering the fight against corruption

The performance of the institutions fighting corruption has been severely hindered by man factors. These include the culture of condoning corruption by the public, inadequate law and poor enforcement of the laws that are in existence, excessive bureaucracy, inadequate funding, the absence of a Government system to co-ordinate the struggle against corruption.

In addition, the performance of the anti-corruption agencies, such as the IGG, DPP, CID and AG has been hampered by under staffing, inadequate training and poorly motivated staff, inadequate logistical support, and following the decentralization, inadequate or total lack of offices at the district levels. Under funding these institutions has continuously incapacitated these agencies ability to address these problems and effectively undertake their operations.

The role of the office of the Vice President

Under Article 108 of the Constitution, the Vice President shall deputise for the President, and perform other functions as may by assigned to him/her by the President under the Constitution. The President in exercise of these powers, assigned the Vice President the task of overseeing the fight against corruption, as the campaign against corruption had not reached the desired level.

To assist the Vice President in this work, an Anti Corruption Unit was established in March 1996. The Cabinet endorsed the unit, in February 1997 and mandated it to co-ordinate the Anti Corruption activities and play a public relations role. The office of the Vice President is also constrained by inadequate resources for recurrent and development expenditure. Adequate resources will need to be secured to achieve the enormous task of co-ordinating the fight against corruption.

Government's ultimate goal
The ultimate goal of government in fighting corruption is to create a corrupt free society. Combating corruption will enable government to finance development programs for the benefit of all Ugandans.

Strategies
To achieve the above goal, the office of the Vice President will use the following strategies;

- A sector by sector based approach will be used to co-ordinate the anti-corruption agencies to ensure that they perform their work. Under this approach the office of the Vice President will also co-ordinate all anti-corruption activities in the country.

- The capacity of the anti-corruption institutions will be strengthened in terms of staffing, training, and logistics and their operations will be reviewed to ensure their effectiveness and efficiency. The remuneration of staff of the anti-corruption agencies will also be improved.

- Government will create a policy and legal framework and that can prevent corruption. This will involve establishing and reviewing policies and laws that relate to anti-corruption and ensure their enforcement through the creation of special courts.

- Government will sensitise and mobilise the public to play its vital role in combating corruption, by reporting corrupt officials and increasing pressure on leaders.

- Government will cooperate with other governments and other international agencies to adopt measures that will address corruption in tendering and procurement, and will lead to the inclusion of anti-corruption clauses in all its contracts. It will also share information with countries that have made progress in combating corruption. Funding to support anti-corruption activities will also be sought.

- Ethical and moral values in society will be strengthened in a bid to develop an anti-corruption culture. Towards this end government will promote transparency and accountability on the part of leaders and those holding public offices, support the development of Codes of Conduct for all professions to combat tendencies in professionals

- Government will promote the creation of a National Integrity Movement at national and grass-roots levels.

- Government will also inculcate an anti-corruption culture in the youth by introducing courses on anti-corruption in the school curriculum.

The anti-corruption programme will need to be sustained. This will require a strong political will, a co-ordinating machinery that enjoys the political clout, availability of resources, committed and qualified staff; the goodwill of the public, and a conducive political environment. It is in light of this government position that I welcome the publication of this book.

PREFACE

Corruption, like most evils, is native to man's heart. It springs up naturally like the weeds that seek to choke crops in every garden, like the dirt that accumulates around every human habitation, like the bacteria that floats in the air we breathe. Its destructive powers have to be contained through deliberate and persistent efforts. Without such efforts, corruption spreads and threatens the survival of organisations and states.

Africa is one of the regions of the world where corruption still flourishes. It has been provided with adequate nutrients by authoritarian governments, by a poorly developed press, by an ill informed public and by lack of a democratic tradition which alone provides checks and balances in the exercise of power by governments.

During the 1990s, however, significant political and economic changes have taken place on the continent, pointing to the possibility of a new era of improved governance, better economic management, and transparency in the way governments conduct their business. From all corners of the continent, authoritarian governments have been given notice that the people are no longer prepared to acquiesce to being exploited and misruled by governments that are not accountable to them.

The cold war was one of the major obstacles that hindered the emergence of democratic governance in Africa as major powers propped up regimes that lost support at home. Such regimes which owed their survival to foreign military support had no reason to be transparent or accountable. They thus used unethical means to buy supporters, to silence or even eliminate opponents while ignoring the legitimate aspirations of the people.

The end of the cold war has created a new atmosphere of openness and transparency in which international cooperation in the fight against corruption has become possible. Such cooperation has become particularly urgent because economic globalisation has made corruption a transnational phenomenon. The conspiracy of silence that existed in many countries a decade ago is giving way to a free exchange of information about the various forms of corrupt practices, their origins and possible ways of combating them. This exchange of information by different actors in the struggle against corruption creates the possibility of developing a wide repertoire of strategies from which different countries can develop models suitable for their own particular countries.

Uganda is one of several African countries where the political leadership has expressed a firm desire to participate in the fight against corruption. This commitment has been expressed by strengthening the investigative machinery of government as well as the judicial system, through according due weight and authority to the Public Accounts Committee of Parliament, through the creation of the office of the Inspector General Government, and most of all, through adoption of a leadership code under which public officials are expected to declare their wealth annually. In addition, a free and vocal press has been permitted to emerge and to inform the public about the wrong doings in high offices.

It was against this background that a seminar for representatives of the integrity system in the country was convened by the Inspector General of Government in December 1974. The meeting became a ground breaking gathering during which key stakeholders in the anti-corruption struggle shared experiences from a wide variety of perspectives and explored ways of working together to tackle a common enemy. The seminar led to a workshop which was organised in November 1995 and during which an action plan and an integrity declaration were made.

The essays which appear in this volume are selected from contributions to both the seminar and the workshop. They range from the critical voices of academicians and journalists to the anguish of investigators and to reflections on the ethics of accountability, transparency and the civic obligations of citizens. They also include reports from Transparency International, about experiences gathered across the globe in the anti-corruption struggle.

It is hoped that these essays will help to enlighten the reader about the diverse manifestations of corruption and how the scourge can be combated.

Editors

Part One

BUILDING INTEGRITY: GENERAL PERSPECTIVES

1 Background to the Integrity System

Augustine Ruzindana

This book records the progress made to date by Uganda's National Integrity Committee in working collectively to overhaul and strengthen key aspects of our country's integrity system.

The committee had its origins in the recognition by the Government of Uganda that the success of our wide-ranging process of major civil service reforms would turn on our ability to achieve a results-orientation on the part of our public service, and that the determining factors in this would be our capacity to deliver these services coupled with the integrity of the individuals and the processes involved. So the issue of integrity—already recognised by our government as a matter of high priority for its social values—was also viewed as being utilitarian: without integrity, services to the public would inevitably suffer and the effectiveness of our wide-ranging reforms would be seriously eroded. The three watchwords for our reform process became "capacity," "integrity" and "results orientation."

In December, 1994, as the Inspector General of Government, I brought together various stakeholders in our national integrity system, with the aim of establishing mechanisms for all of us to work together in an integrated and holistic fashion. As we discussed the various challenges which each of us, individually, faced, it became apparent it was necessary not only to agree on an action plan, assigning targets and responsibilities, but also to establish an organisational framework through which progress could be reviewed and the action plan developed in the light of evolving circumstances.

The stakeholders at this initial meeting included parliamentarians (including a member of the Public Accounts Committee), the Auditor-

General, the Director of Public Prosecutions as well as the Ministries of Public Service, Education, and Information. Also represented was the civil society in the form of the newly established national chapter of Transparency International, Transparency-Uganda. Some of those present (including my own Office) enjoy constitutional independence, but none of those involved allowed this status to constrain a meaningful and creative debate.

The action plan which we developed during the seminar was wide-ranging, touching on matters affecting prevention, enforcement, capacity-building and public awareness. We recognised that it could not be implemented overnight and that each of us would need some time to address the targets we had set. The stakeholders met collectively for a second time in November 1995, to take stock of progress made and to further develop the action plan. Also added to our committee on this occasion was the Central Tender Board, in recognition of its centrality in government procurement and the need to ensure that tendering under our decentralisation programme is rendered fair, open and competitive, and represents value for money.

As this volume of essays shows, the progress made has been substantial, and each of us came away with a shared feeling of having taken a significant step forward. This is not to suggest that all of our targets proved realistic within the time-frame allowed. Much more remains to be done. The committee was emboldened by the successes attained and it went ahead to define new targets.

A special feature of our second meeting was the realisation that all of us should publicly commit ourselves to the tasks we had in hand. This, we felt, would serve three objectives. First, it would assist in the raising of public awareness; second, it would draw public attention to our work; and third, in the context of the approaching elections, it would provide a platform for us to seek public endorsement of our goals from candidates of whatever political persuasion. The declaration we made at the end of our meeting has since received widespread publicity on both radio and in the press.

Another important feature was the presence of a number of journalists throughout our deliberations. We recognised that the public interest would best be served by our discussions being frank and open, and that public confidence in the processes would best be fostered by the knowledge of what was being done, why it was being done and where the difficulties might lie. One of our initial objectives had been to promote the training of investigative journalists (in recognition of the important role which a free press has to play in helping to secure and maintain the integrity of public servants and public institutions), and those attending a week-long training course organised by my Office were invited to sit in, and report on our deliberations. This helped to consolidate the confidence we have sought to build between key public servants and the press as well as bring about the realisation on the part of the mass media of some of the complexities and challenges with which we are all faced.

The task of building an integrity system which will serve Uganda and all Ugandans well is one of the highest national priorities. But we also recognise that it is a task which, even when our major work is done, is one which will still require constant attention to keep our relevant institutions and practices in line with changing conditions and with emerging new knowledge.

We are, ourselves, quietly proud of the part which we played in addressing national challenges in this holistic and co-operative fashion, particularly as it is one which we believe to be unique in Africa, and perhaps in the wider world. We intend to continue with our efforts to ensure that all Ugandans have a public service of which they can be justly proud, and that all members of the public service can be seen as being of manifest integrity.

2 The National Integrity System in Uganda

James Katorobo

Introduction

During the colonial and early post-colonial period cases of embezzlement and corruption were rare. Administrative ethics required officials to declare and surrender to the state any gifts they received. Financial standing orders regarding accounting for imprest and advances were respected and followed. Books of account were properly kept up to date and maintained. These high standards of public morality were eroded during the period of political instability and administrative decay. The violation of Asian property rights in the confiscation and expulsion of 1972 led to generalised disrespect for property rights. Graft and corruption became uncontrolled channels to political and economic power.

Macro and microeconomic mismanagement, for example, overvalued currencies, and shortage of commodities resulted in a speculative economy. Petty trading in an economy of shortages was more rewarding than hard work. A get-rich-quick mentality became entrenched. Most of the methods and practices that it encouraged undermined the standing orders that had been the cornerstone of public morality.

The scope for corrupt behaviour expanded when the number of public enterprises grew threefold, local government centres were destroyed, and power was centralised. Furthermore, the machinery for inspection and supervision broke down and, finally, accounting and enforcement of morality collapsed. Rampant corruption had become such a major issue that it qualified as part of the ten-point programme of the NRM government.

The political response to the loss of public service integrity was to raise the issue of corruption to the top ten issues on the NRM agenda for action. The NRM government adopted a two-pronged attack on corruption involving the enactment of an anti-corruption law, the leadership code, and establishing an anti-corruption office – the Office of the Inspector General of Government (IGG).

These initiatives were very important. But their effectiveness was reduced by the policy of reconciliation which led government to be less vigorous in enforcing the leadership code. Even when the Public Service Review and Re-organisation Commission (PSRRC) (1990) recommended anti-corruption measures, including the establishment of an administrative code of conduct, very little progress was achieved in this direction. It was against this background that the office of the IGG, in collaboration with the Economic Development Institute (EDI) of the World Bank, organised a workshop on Designing a Programme to Enhance Ethics, Transparency and Accountability in Uganda (9-10 December 1994).

The components of a programme to promote national integrity were agreed upon at the workshop on Designing a Programme to Enhance Ethics, Transparency and Accountability in Uganda (9–10 December 1994). This was the first integrity workshop run by the office of the IGG in collaboration with the EDI of the World Bank. "To have an honest and responsible public sector which will uphold professional ethics, be transparent and accountable in its work" was adopted but it was realised that some of the reform measures would be long term and would require a lot of resources to be mobilised. Consequently, participants agreed to adopt a minimal short-term achievable programme.

Awareness

These objectives focused on the creation of awareness and the promotion of quick return improvements in the existing anti-corruption machinery. The one-year targets included conducting anti-corruption awareness workshops for strategically selected opinion leaders in the country. These workshops were conducted for central ministries, district government staff, political leaders, permanent secretaries, the managers of enforcement institutions (legal, police, prisons). A major component of the programme targeted the mass media (training in investigative journalism) and other elements of civil society.

Enforcement

Special initial targets were directed at improving enforcement of existing anti-corruption measures:

- Setting up a special court to deal with corruption cases
- Delegating DPP powers to IGG staff to prosecute
- Establishing a mechanism for random checking to ensure compliance with existing ethical codes
- Prosecution of outstanding corruption and fraud cases
- Freezing, seizing and confiscating proceeds of corruption and fraud
- Enforcing the Prevention of Corruption Act of 1970 taking advantage of provisions that shift the burden of proof to the accused
- Ensuring that books of accounts in ministries and districts are completed before March 1995.

Institution building

Emphasis has been put on the breakdown of institutions and systems as a main cause for the erosion of integrity. Therefore a key solution in the restoration of integrity is institution and capacity building. It was therefore imperative to strengthen relevant agencies engaged in investigation and enforcement, for example, the IGG, Attorney General, DPP, CID, Customs, Inspectors in Ministries, and so on.

Publications

A key weapon in the fight against corruption is adequate and relevant information conveyed to the right consumers at the right time. The programme had the target of:

(i) generating and distributing information to public servants on corruption as well as standing orders
(ii) development of ethics training materials for schools, media, and religious institutions
(iii) designing multi-media ethics information including theatrical performances, radio programmes, popular competitions, and so on.

The achievements of the first one -year programme to enhance ethics and promote accountability

The achievements of the first-year programme were presented and discussed at the November 27–28 1995 Mukono National Integrity Workshop. Each of the targets were reviewed. The level of achievement was very high, reflecting realism in setting the objectives and committed implementation on the part of the office of the IGG, the donors and the World Bank. The only area of performance below target was the publication objective. This has now been rescheduled. In assessing the issue of publications, it is important to note that the programme encouraged papers to be written for the workshops. These papers and the workshop proceedings have been printed and widely distributed.

The objective of institution and capacity building with respect to the restoration of existing institutions were carried out. For example, ODA assistance has been used to build a training unit for the IGG and to improve police training and renovate and re-equip the judiciary. Perhaps the most notable achievement is the establishment of a Ugandan chapter of Transparency International.

One of the achievements of the first phase of the national integrity programme was the course to enhance investigative journalism skills. In any society the mass media is a key pillar of democracy and accountability. It is an institution that is often harassed and crippled by dictatorial regimes. It was therefore a wise move to put in place measures to enhance the capacity of journalists to play their role in exposing corruption.

The way forward

The fight against corruption has been stepped up by increasing the enforcement powers of the IGG and entrenching those powers in the new constitution (Chapters 13 and 14). We may expect vigorous and more sustained enforcement of public morality. The Leadership Code will be enforced, especially the provision regarding declaration of assets. It will be essential to consolidate and expand the scope of the anti-corruption measures launched during the first year, especially the enhancement of investigation and enforcement.

3 Elements of a Successful Anti-Corruption Strategy

Jeremy Pope

Why fight corruption at all?

Combating corruption is not an end in itself. Rather it is instrumental to the broader goal of more effective, fair and efficient government. Anti-corruption activists are not just concerned singly with corruption, but with its impact on development and society. How does corruption impact on poverty alleviation through distorting developmental decision-making? How inefficient is bribery? Who ultimately ends up paying the cost of corruption?

Although corruption itself is costly, it would not be worthwhile to attempt to eliminate it entirely. Under many realistic conditions, it would simply be too expensive to reduce corruption to zero, let alone the negative impact it would have on other freedoms and fundamental human rights that would be constrained and intruded upon unreasonably and unacceptably. Programme elimination may be unjustified, bureaucratic discretion may be necessary for effective administration, stronger enforcement and deterrence may be expensive. Thus, the aim is not to achieve complete rectitude, but rather a fundamental increase in the honesty—and so the efficiency and fairness—of government.

Although background conditions in societies vary greatly, in every one the basic policy responses to corruption are likely to be of three types: substantive, structural and moral. In their totality, and each individually, they unite the interests and involvement of government, the private sector and civil society.

Some lessons from the past

TI's analysis of the successes (comparatively rare) and the failures (numerous) of past efforts in various countries identifies the several elements. Limits of power exist at the top. An incoming administration may have wished to tackle corruption effectively but, through inheriting a corrupt bureaucracy, the very corruption in that bureaucracy has impeded efforts for change. There also has been an absence of commitment at the top. Overlay ambitious promises have led to unrealistic and unachievable expectations and a consequent loss of public confidence. Reforms have been "piecemeal" and uncoordinated – no one has "owned" the reforms, been committed to them and been driven to see the reforms implemented and kept up to date. Reforms have relied too much upon the law – an uncertain instrument for changing the way in which people behave – or too much on enforcement, leading to repression, apparent abuses of enforcement power and the emergence of further corruption. Reforms have "overlooked" those at the top and focused only on the "small fry." The law, if applied unfairly and unevenly, soon ceases to be applied at all. Also, reforms have lacked a specific focus and, in failing to deliver any "quick wins", have quickly lost public support. Even where reforms have been focused and changes real, they have not endured where institutional mechanisms do not outlive the leaders of the reforms. Above all, an attempt by the government alone to achieve reforms without drawing in the actors best able to assist it from civil society and the private sector.

An overall strategy

The development of a coherent, overall, holistic strategy involves a clear commitment by political leaders to combat corruption wherever it occurs (and submitting themselves to scrutiny). Primary attention should be given to prevention of future corruption and changing systems (rather than indulging in witch-hunts and so on). A comprehensive anti-corruption legislation should be adopted and implemented by agencies of manifest integrity (including investigators, prosecutors and adjudicators). Areas of government activity most prone to corruption should be identified and relevant procedures reviewed as a matter of priority. It should be ensured that the salaries of civil servants and political leaders adequately reflect the responsibilities of the posts and as comparable as possible with those in the private sector (both to reduce the "need" for corruption and to ensure that the best are available to serve the state. Legal and administrative remedies should provide an adequate deterrence (for example corruption-induced contracts rendered void and unenforceable; closely monitoring large transactions; random intensive audits; rendering licences and permits obtained through corruption void). A creative partnership should be forged between government and civil society, including the private sector, the professions, religious organisations and so on. Reforms may be conceptualised under the four headings of prevention, enforcement, public awareness, and institution building. At the end of the day, corruption should be– and be seen as – a "high risk" and "low profit" undertaking.

Prevention (Reducing Opportunities for Corruption)

Steps to simplify government programmes and procedures will help to reduce the opportunities for corruption. First, the more efficient the design of a programme, the less prone to corruption it will be, for example, by eliminating "gatekeepers" in a position to exact tolls from users. The number of steps required to gain government approvals and payments for goods supplied should be reduced. A radical simplification and enforcement of regulations should not simply diminish the need for people to resort to bribery but also ease the transaction of business of all sorts and of people's access to public services generally. Finally, payrolls should be cleaned up in order to eliminate "ghosts" and render their reappearance more difficult.

Areas of discretion should be minimised and, where possible, eliminated. If such areas are retained, officials should be given clear guidelines in writing as to how these are to be exercised, and the guidelines published.

Opportunities for corruption will also be reduced through the demystification of government since corruption thrives where the public do not know their rights. Materials such as staff manuals should be published and made accessible to department users, and so on. Improved work methods and procedures will reduce delay.

Another means of reducing the opportunities for corruption is the depersonalisation of government by minimising face-to-face contact. Random elements should be introduced so that users cannot predict the officials with whom they may be dealing. Also, staff should be rotated regularly to minimise the scope for unhealthy relationships developing, both between individual staff and the public they are serving, and within "groups" in particular areas of government service.

Examination should be made of mechanisms available to provide speedy and effective reviews of contentious decisions. Managers at all levels should be responsible for the activities of subordinates. This can be achieved through the increased effectiveness of supervision to enable superior officers to check and control the work of their staff. Also, surprise checks should be made on the work of officers, and officials at management levels should regularly certify compliance with civil service regulations and the law by those underneath them.

Assets, incomes and liabilities of officials with decision-making powers (to ensure that these are consistent with known income and reasonable expectations) and appropriate bans on post-public employment by the private sector should be monitored effectively.

Complaint channels that enable junior officials to complain about their superiors' corruption should be organised and the press should be guaranteed the freedom to expose corruption.

Although the fight against corruption is not the primary task of privatisation, it can lead to a reduction in opportunities for corrupt activities. Of course the process of privatisation requires special measures of transparency to ensure that the process itself is kept reasonably clean.

Rewards for achievement, including the recognition and rewarding of good behaviour, should be implemented. Role models should be acclaimed. Mechanisms for civil society should be established and should feed in to a continuous process of review. The public should be polled periodically in order to gauge its perceptions of change. Arrangements should be made for the payment of a living wage in line with reasonable needs and expectations.

It is important to create an open, genuinely competitive and transparent system of public procurement. To reinforce anti-corruption efforts, professional bodies (accountants, auditors, lawyers) should declare participation in corrupt activities (including money-laundering) to be unprofessional activities and their members liable to be professionally barred. The reporting of all gifts, hospitality and so on received by government officials should be required, as well as the reporting and recording of all political donations.

It is necessary to review and enforce appropriate "conflict of interest" regulations, including the introduction of ethics programmes and periodic group discussions of real-life ethical dilemmas drawn from their own experiences. Where necessary, removing certain activities from the mainstream of the public service should be considered in order to enable, among other things, better salaries to be paid there without distorting civil service relativities (for example constituting a separate revenue authority). The removal of "monopolies" within the bureaucracy is important in order to provide rival sources, for example, drivers' licences, thereby ending unofficial "charges" or at least to drive the "price" down. Also, coalitions of interests in support of corruption prevention should be built, drawing in the private sector and civil society.

Enforcement (Increasing Likelihood of Corruption Being Detected and Punished)

Independent mechanisms should be implemented such as investigators, prosecutors, adjudicators who are able to perform their professional duties in a transparently independent fashion, and to enforce the rule of law against all who breach it, whatever their positions (and depoliticising law enforcement). Adequate powers of investigation and prosecution consistent with international human rights norms will be necessary including:

- access to all government documentation;
- placing the onus of proving legitimate acquisition of wealth on the person who has it;
- giving investigators access to records held by lawyers and financial advisers; and
- developing sound arrangements for international mutual legal assistance with relevant countries.

Provisions should be made for transparent mechanisms lifting any immunities which high public officials may enjoy by reason of their office. The establishment of channels for effective complaint-making, whether by whistle blowers (within and from departments) or by members of the public, should also be provided because it is essential that neither feels unnecessarily exposed to reprisals. Examples of such channels include: telephone "hotlines" and counselling (preferably from outside the civil service).

When necessary, physical witness protection for key witnesses should be provided, whether inside or outside the country.

Mechanisms for punishing those outside the jurisdiction should be developed. The use of civil penalties should be considered (which, as judgements of the ordinary courts, may be enforced abroad) whereas criminal sanctions generally cannot. Also, the blacklisting of corrupt firms and sales-staff should be considered (and publication of these as a way of ensuring that other countries—and competitors—are aware of the corrupt activities). Extradition arrangements should be ensured so that corrupt officials who flee will be returned by court order from the most attractive countries of refuge. Legal provisions should be implemented which enable the profits of the corrupt to be seized and forfeited, whether these be inside or outside the country.

Ordinary civil courts should be used by empowering private interests to sue for damages where they lose money and contracts through the corrupt activities of others.

Public Awareness

Public understanding should be engendered regarding:

- the harm done by corruption;
- the fact that the corrupt are stealing the public's money;
- their rights to services—at a given price or at no cost at all; and
- their duty to complain when officials behave corruptly in specific cases and how this should be done.

Public perceptions of existing levels of corruption should be ascertained as well as where it is taking place to provide a base line against which progress can be measured. Legal and administrative environment must provide an enabling environment for a free press through the following:

- Freedom of information laws;
- review defamation laws and "insult" laws to ensure that these cannot be used unreasonably to threaten and fetter the press (that is public figures, as legitimate objects of public interest, should enjoy less protection than ordinary private citizens);
- no censorship;
- professional standards raised;
- no discrimination against newspapers through withdrawals of government advertising, through access to newsprint and so on; and
- ensure state-owned media employees can maintain professional standards of independence and responsibility.

The environment in which civil society operates must be appropriate for a free and democratic society, for instance, registration provisions must exist and should be simple and inexpensive, and registration should be a right, not a privilege.

Institution Building

First, all relevant institutions must be adequately staffed and resourced. Investigations and prosecutions must be conducted independently. Certain questions must be answered, including:

- Is there a need for an Independent Commission Against Corruption?
- Are laws of evidence appropriate to a modern era?
- Are penalties too low (not deterrent) or too high (deterrent to prosecutions being brought)?

A review of internal financial management systems must be made to ensure adequacy and effectiveness.

The Auditor General must ensure the independence of, among other things, a thorough appointing mechanism; widespread publicity for reports; action to implement recommendations; and independence and professionalism.

The Ombudsman, or the equivalent office, should have adequate powers; be able to ensure response to recommendations; publicise existence of office; and publicise reports by office.

The Contractor-General must establish the need for an independent oversight of government contracting and his/her performance thereafter. The office must ensure capacity for independent oversight and evaluation and public reporting of what is taking place with public contracts and their implementation.

Procurement must be professionalised by examining present practices against "best practice" and most transparent systems. Choice must not be captive to departmental advice and interests, and the involvement of "outsiders" should be an integral part. Decision-makers should be pooled with no predictability as to who will be involved in any particular exercise. Speedy decision-making should be enforced to eliminate delay during which corruption can take place, and regular scrutiny (and complaints-based scrutiny) of departmental procedures should occur.

A review of training needs should be conducted including:

- in-service training for civil servants at all levels together with the formulation and dissemination of clearly defined ethical guidelines and rules of conduct; and
- review of training needs of all relevant departments and agencies.

Access to the courts for purposes of remedying complaints should be simplified and the adequacy of judicial review of administrative action should be ensured.

The Electoral Commission should be guaranteed independence, impartiality and public and political party confidence and should maintain transparency in all aspects of elections system (except, of course, the ballot). The commission should foster public participation in the monitoring process to build confidence and train not only its own staff but also political party officials in order to ensure familiarity with the system and enable them to monitor it professionally.

Legislative mechanisms for accountability including the role of the Public Accounts Committee should be reviewed and revised. Public access to proceedings should be maximised. A capacity for regular polling of the public should be developed.

Next steps

Possible Next Steps Include:

A national integrity working group should be established, however described or constituted, drawing together all the stakeholders within government (executive office, public service, investigation, prosecution, judiciary, education, information and key vulnerable departments such as customs, procurement, revenue collection, local government) together with coalition partners from outside government (civil society, religious leaders, the private sector, relevant professional bodies—law, auditing, accounting and including health professionals—and groups representing consumer interests).

The existing framework should be analysed and areas of reform identified.

An overall plan which includes short-term, medium-term and long-term goals (including a public awareness-raising programme), and assigns responsibilities for follow-up action and reporting back to the working group should be developed.

The establishment of the working group as well as its overall plan should be published. Inputs from the wider public will be solicited in such a manner. The endorsement of the plan by the political leadership and its public backing of the work to be done should also be published.

Regular meetings of the working group and appropriate publicity to its work should occur with particular attention being paid to achieving some "quick wins" to build public confidence.

Five final thoughts

1. Reform is a long-term process where attitudes and conduct must be taught and reinforced at all levels;
2. Reform should initially only tackle issues where it can be most effective or where there is the most added value;
3. Reform is a question of fashioning building blocks which must be put in place over a number of years;
4. The process of, and commitment to, reform must be owned visibly, and supported from the top; and
5. Tackling corruption is not just about tackling corruption: It is about the public's confidence in, and loyalty to, the State—and the State's financial and policy abilities to reciprocate.

Part Two

CORRUPTION IN UGANDA

4 Corruption in the Public Service: An Assessment

[This is extract is Chapter 14 of the Report of the Public Service Review and Reorganisation Commission of Uganda 1989/90]

Introduction

Public Service Review and Reorganisation Commission terms of reference were as follows

The Commission's Terms of Reference require us:

a. To examine the causes of inefficiency in the Public Service, and propose solutions thereto;

b. To examine and propose ways and means of improving the morale of officers in the Public Service;

c. To inquire into any other matter connected or incidental to the above terms.

It is indisputable that lack of tools, funds, equipment, office space and transport are a major cause of inefficiency. It is also agreed that the incredibly meagre salaries and poor conditions of service as well as insecurity of tenure have a lot to do with low morale throughout the Service. Nevertheless, related to both is the problem of corruption in public life which, by its all-pervasive incidence, constitutes an important contributory factor in both inefficiency and low morale.

From this perspective it can be argued that even if salaries and conditions of service of public employees were improved; and needed tools, funds and equipment were provided; the services rendered to society would not improve much so long as corruption remained the major problem that it has been for the last 2 years. That there is serious corruption in all segments and at all levels of the public service cannot be disputed, as evidenced by the reports of the Pubic Accounts Committee (PAC), the Auditor General, the Inspector-General of Government as well as reports and readers' comments in the press.

Definition of corruption

It is easy to reach a consensus on the existence of corruption in the public service. But when it comes to stating the precise nature of the practice, we have a real definitional problem.

Some instances have the appearance of innocent traditional practices carried over into modern bureaucracy. Others appear to be straightforward fraud such as false claims; or a mere weak administration and poor accountability, including failure to account for advances and allowances on completion of a trip, among other things. It can also include cases of sheer wasteful expenditure: for example, unnecessary and excessively large delegations on trips abroad, membership or size of which has nothing to do with the official objective of the trips. Others are more obviously "corruption" as popularly understood, that is, straightforward bribery. But basic to all the instances that can be cited is this one element: that, somehow, their official capacity allows considerations other than those of probity, strict accountability, efficiency and economy to influence or distort their decision-making and action.

The Inspector-General of Government, in a paper on "Corruption and Mismanagement in Government" presented at a Seminar on Uganda's Economy held in Kampala (12-16 December, 1989) depicted the problem thus:

> Corruption is difficult to define but everybody knows and understands what it is, though attitudes for or against it differ from person to person and from society to society. Corruption could be called any practice or act or omission, by a public official that is a deviation from the norm and that cannot be openly acknowledged but must be hidden from the public eye. Corruption diverts official decision-making from what a decision should have been to what it should not have been. Corruption introduces discrimination and arbitrariness in decision-making so that rules, regulations and procedures become unimportant. In the extreme cases decision-making is not only transferred to the corrupters but it is totally hijacked by, and arrogated to the corrupters. Where countries are concerned, sovereignty is completely surrendered.

More specifically, corruption is defined as a conduct or practice by a public official or private individual done in flagrant violation of existing rules and procedures for the realisation of personal or group gains. Corruption takes many forms including bribery, unofficial commissions, kick-backs and pay-offs, purchase and sale of "air," embezzlement, and so on.

In this part of our report, we have confined our attention to the Public Service as simply defined in our terms of reference, and have not inquired into or commented on the military, parastatals or public political life—all of which are commonly known to be equally afflicted by corruption.

Causes of corruption

Given the nature and scope of the problem, the next concern is to find out the underlying causes—direct or indirect—as well as other contributory factors.

i. *Income-Expenditure gap in Uganda*

The current extremely low salaries/wages paid to members of the Public Service can be taken as the number one contributory factor to corruption. The lowest paid staff, according to the Circular Standing Instruction No. 6 of 1990, is paid a salary of only Ushs. 2,591 per month (about US$ 5.8 at the current official exchange rate of 450/= to US$ 1).

The highest paid official receives a salary of UShs 12,155 per month equivalent to US$ 27.0. It is true that most of the senior staff in addition benefit from rent-free furnished houses, use of official vehicles, as well as monthly responsibility allowances. However, the extremely low salaries make it impossible for the majority of staff to meet their daily basic needs, for example education of their children, feeding, clothing and taking care of the medical needs of themselves and their families. This has for a long time been a major contributory factor to widespread corruption. The Commission addresses the remuneration issue in detail in Chapter 15. (See the Report)

ii. *Shortages and monopoly*

For many years Uganda has faced severe shortages of consumer goods, limited access to major imported articles, foreign currency, and so on which necessitated considerable central control and regulations. These restrictions gave public officers and others in positions of influence unlimited discretionary powers to render or withhold service, or to control purchases of goods which were in great demand. Members of the public, anxious to secure the scarce resources and needed services, quickly realised that the only way to achieve their objective was to offer bribes.

iii. *Broad discretionary Powers*

As explained above, public officials are given or acquire personalised political and administrative powers which they use (or withhold) in return for favours or support. Quite often such powers are used to protect their friends, relations, the unfit, the corrupt or straightforward thieves, thus encouraging more corruption. Power so vested in or grabbed by individual officials is seldom effectively supervised and is therefore invariably used contrary to laid down rules and regulations. The resulting adverse impact on the efficiency of the service is obvious; because unless certain officers are "seen" (bribed) nothing can be done, even when they are not available in the office.

iv. *Weak administrative controls*

Cases have been reported many times of senior public officials embezzling huge amounts of public funds intended to pay staff salaries and allowances, finance projects, or for the repair of government vehicles. In other cases officials have embezzled hospital drugs and equipment or have signed inflated purchase and procurement contracts for commissions paid in overseas bank accounts. Until the advent of the NRM Government, the Public Accounts Committee was in limbo and the annual Auditor-General's Reports were completely and contemptuously ignored. This lack of accountability resulted in officials misappropriating public funds with impunity, knowing that they will not be asked to account for the money under their control; or they could always plead that the documents were looted or were missing. Another example of lack of a corrective mechanism has been exemplified in the now widespread practice of using cash rather than Local Purchase Orders backed by payment vouchers and cheques as required in the financial regulations. The general breakdown of controls, making it difficult or impossible to keep track of administrative transactions, has contributed most to the proliferation of corruption in the Service.

v. *Complex and cumbersome bureaucracy*

Unnecessarily cumbersome, complicated and often unwritten procedures result in long delays in rendering what would normally be a straightforward service, for example, issuing of renewed drivers' licences, registration of vehicles, clearance of imports and approval of bank loans. To circumvent the resulting unnecessary delays, members of the public are made to know that the problems would disappear if they paid "chai" (tea) or "coughed", that is if they paid money to the corrupt officials concerned. These types of corruption are very widespread, ranging from the smallest service, for example, when renewing a vehicle registration, to big cases, such as when purchasing and leasing plots of land or subsidised trucks or tractors.

vi. *Insecure or precarious tenure of office*

Quite often people in top positions, whether politicians or public servants, feel insecure and threatened by the possibility that they could be removed from their "eating" (profitable) offices any time. Often these officials are insecure because they lack the basic qualification for the position, or were wrongly appointed to the posts through political patronage or on sectarian grounds and so on. Consequently they try to grab as much as they can within the shortest possible time.

They demand big bribes, commissions and kick-backs; or engage in downright plunder to amass wealth while they have the opportunity—so that they can live quite comfortably if they get thrown out of office. Their colleagues and junior staff, observing that the bosses are looting with impunity, quickly follow the example; and corruption gets institutionalised in the Service. Very soon, members of the public learn that if you want quick service, or any service from certain offices, you have to bribe key individuals.

vii. *Personal greed/ambition*

Some public officials simply have an unrestrained desire to get rich quickly by fair or foul means. It is immaterial how much salary they are paid; such grabbers will never be paid enough. Officials who steal millions of shillings in one position and continue to steal even bigger amounts on transfer to other positions cannot plead low salaries or survival reasons to justify their corruption. Theirs becomes something almost akin to kleptomania, as if by nature they cannot help being corrupt.

viii. *Weak sanctions*

Corruption is present in both developed and developing countries. What makes the difference is the official attitude to it. In some developing countries harsh anti-corruption laws have been enacted. For example, in one West African country, three executives were executed for corruption offences. Consequently, although corruption may not have been eliminated, there is at least a strong deterrent. In Uganda, the legal sanctions are basically in place, that is the Anti-Corruption Law (1970) and various provisions in the Penal Code. However, the sanctions (or fines) that are meted out to both the giver and the recipient of corruption have been so eroded by inflation that they are no longer effective deterrents. Corruption will continue so long as corrupt people are not severely punished. Suspension, transfer and forced retirement are not effective deterrents at all. In addition corruption is difficult to prove in courts of law because of "the satisfied customer" relationship. Quite often, too, the accused uses his ill-gotten loot to hire enable defence counsel or bribe the investigators and police so that the case files disappear. As a result of such manoeuvres either the case collapses or the charge gets so watered down that even where they are convicted the punishment (usually a fine) amounts to little more than a mild slap on the hand.

ix. *Non-recognition/encouragement*

It would be wrong to assume that all public officers are corrupt. Many have valiantly struggled to remain clean. However, the absence of any form of official recognition or encouragement for honest service makes them wonder whether it is worthwhile and whether their honesty will ever be rewarded. Some brave nationalistic officials go to the extent of reporting and documenting corrupt acts by colleagues. Unfortunately the lack of protection for such whistle-blowers has resulted in some being pushed out or transferred to less popular stations, harassed as deviants from the "'normal" behaviour, and in some cases they have been framed up on spurious charges and even dismissed. The basic problem is that such abandonment of whistle-blowers to their fate will discourage others from following their bold example if they come to realise that they will be left to the mercy of the powerful corrupt people whom they had sought to expose.

x. *Systematic/hostile environment*
There are systems or regulations which are so inconvenient and unreasonable that they unwittingly force people to resort to corruption. For example, heavy tax deposits payable even before an investor has done any business, exorbitant fees or high tax levels, unreasonably long waiting periods before one can get certain benefits lead to official enforcement staff bargaining with members of the public so as to reduce or remove the effect of the self-defeating official measure.

Effects of corruption

Corruption adversely affects society and the nation politically, administratively, economically, and socio-culturally.

Political

Corruption increases public cynicism towards the prevailing political system. Due to the loss of respect for the law, open flouting of regulations and consequent ineffectiveness of government, the political philosophies and programmes of those in power tend to lose credibility. Some people in leadership positions continue to preach anti-corruption but go on looting and plundering. They become more determined and ruthless to remain in office, in order to continue eating and to cover up past corruption. These acts eventually undermine the stability and authority of the state itself as has happened in some parts of Latin America, where powerful corrupt barons have been known to hold the state itself to ransom. President Museveni in May 1990 at a press conference expressed concern about corruption which, he said, had now infiltrated the NRM's top leadership and even some institutions responsible for combating corruption. As he lamented, this could seriously undermine the NRM's moral authority to continue fighting corruption at all.

Administrative/Managerial

The impact of corruption on the efficiency of organs of the Public Service has been alluded to above. It distracts the attention of officials from their public functions to activities which would facilitate their private (corrupt) benefit. Some government departments or divisions of the same department become popular because of the "eating" that prevails in them; others are considered "dry" and unpopular because they offer no chances for corrupt practices. Some staff would do anything to stay in Ministries or Departmental Headquarters and resist being posted upcountry, even on promotion, because of the "better" opportunities of "eating" in the capital. The negative impact on the morale of staff who continue to depend on their salaries and allowances makes it difficult for any meaningful work to be performed in some districts. They see so much corruption going on, apparently successfully and with impunity—while they continue to suffer and tighten their belts because they have chosen to remain honest.

Economical/Financial

Corruption in Uganda has resulted in large-scale diversion of resources from the public to individual use. Funds intended to finance critical developmental projects have been, and continue to be, embezzled. Contracts of all types have been inflated and revised many times to ensure payment of huge amounts of commissions to those in official positions to approve or sign such contracts. The traditional and previously well-observed regulations and procedures of contracting have been abandoned. This lack of systemic discipline and checks and balances has led to what the IGG has aptly called "extravagant, conspicuous and uncontrollable expenditure of public funds" and untold haemorrhage of the financial, physical and human resources of the country with "serious devastating effects upon the economy."

Indeed, corruption has resulted in the flight of capital and withholding of loans or aid resources for fear that the loans or funds will not achieve the intended objectives. Corruption, thus, has led to widespread unemployment and poverty.

Socio-Cultural

Corruption dehumanises and erodes respectability of public officers, which paves the way for more blatant corruption and the erosion of morals and ethics in society. The human rights of innocent individuals, especially those of "whistle blowers", are often trampled upon when corrupt law enforcement agencies unjustly punish the innocent, and assist the well-heeled culprits to escape scot-free. People begin to believe that justice is only available to those who can afford to pay the highest bribes or can pull effective political strings to ensure that files disappear and their cases are dismissed. Innocent staff see their colleagues building huge houses, purchasing big vehicles and spending large amounts of money obtained through corruption. Eventually, they too set out to emulate the corrupt ones. The general crimerate goes up, leading to more human rights abuses and general social misery.

Combating corruption

Like all wars, the fight against corruption will be hard and protracted. However, it is a war that must be fought and won. Remedial actions will have to be instituted on various fronts; and some of these are discussed in the paragraphs that follow.

One cause of corruption is the fact that too many activities have been concentrated in government, thereby limiting access and creating the tedious procedures and rigid controls that become an open invitation to corruption. It is noteworthy that if there is only one point for the delivery of a service—even a free service—there will be people prepared to bribe someone to jump the inevitable queue. Certain government activities therefore need to be dispersed; and government can reduce its role in some forms of delivery, where appropriate, by positive encouragement of the private sector to undertake activities that are not inherently governmental.

Control over information is a source of power; and many officials thrive on concealing or hoarding information that should be public in the first place so as to use their new-found power to extort monies from the public. As far as possible all transactions of public business should be de-personalised, in the sense that the customer should not have to contact any particular official for information that could easily be made available through posters and notices on walls or forms and leaflets that could be placed on open counters or shelves. Improving and making transparent administrative systems, procedures and regulations to reduce and eventually eliminate the usual frustrating delays will help to avoid the temptation to demand or offer a consideration to expedite action. For instance, the regulations and procedures required to start a company, to import or export, to register a vehicle, among others, should all be simplified, clearly written and conspicuously displayed in the appropriate offices for the convenience of the public.

The supervisory and inspection roles in the public service need to be strengthened. Many of the Inspectorates in the Civil Service, for instance, are either defunct or completely immobilised—mainly due to shortage of qualified staff or lack of funds, transport and other equipment. As a result, many Public Service activities are not effectively monitored and supervised, if at all. When Inspectors of Schools are unable, for lack of transport, to go into the field for years on end, is it any wonder that unscrupulous officials succeed in siphoning off millions of shillings in respect of schools that in fact do not exist?

Perhaps the best case for the improvement and tightening of controls and random spot-checks or inspections can be found in the operations regarding group employees. The biggest loophole conducive to corruption is the unrestricted freedom given to senior officers to recruit non-established group employees. Being temporary employees, this category of staff are hired and fired at will. Since funds for their wages are released in lump-sum, unmatched to any staff lists, corrupt officials routinely exploit the situation by manipulating the numbers and inflating the wage bill to cover non-existent "ghost" workers—pocketing the surplus funds or paying some of it out to friends and relatives and so on who just turn up on pay day to collect their pay.

That the absence of controls in the operation of the group employee system has become a big corruption racket is dramatically demonstrated by the recent experience of Kampala City Council. It is significant that in a recent exercise requiring all the Council's group employees to collect their pay from a special desk manned by neutral (that is previously unknown) accounts staff, Kampala City Council was able to save UShs 6 million from uncollected wages; and a total of UShs 11 million was saved on the wage bill for just one month, the results of "ghosts" scared off by the trap. Obviously, it does not require the service of an exorcist to rid the Service of "ghost workers." Administrative lapses are the cause of the phenomenon; and it only requires imaginative application of effective administrative controls to effect a cure.

In private business, it is axiomatic that "money begets money." One spends money (free samples, clearance sales, open days, "give-away" prizes, sponsorship of charities and events, and lavish advertisements and so on) in order to pull in more money in the long run. Oddly enough, Government, the biggest business of all, does not appear to believe in this principle. The most astonishing thing is the way in which even revenue-generating agencies are denied the most basic "tools" of their trade because of "lack of funds." Thus, many revenue collecting points in the entire public service system go for months, if not years, without official receipt books, leaving the field open to unscrupulous employees to issue fictitious receipts written on scraps of paper for huge sums of money which they seldom account for afterwards.

It is time Government stopped this "penny – wise, pound-foolish" approach to managing public business. If the Government Printer is given the funds to print adequate quantities of the various receipt books and forms of all kinds necessary for the transaction of Government business in all offices, not only will this yield dividends through vastly improved revenue collection, but it will also plug many of the loopholes for corruption in the Service.

The notoriously long time-lag in the preparation of annual reports of all kinds in the public service provides a convenient cover for corrupt practices. In some cases by the time murky details of some transactions come to light, it is too late to save the situation. It is therefore important for Government to insist on scrupulous and prompt accounting and publication of annual audits for government departments and government-funded agencies. In this respect, the point of the preceding paragraph is pertinent. If institutions like the Auditor-General and the various Inspectorates are starved of the funds required for requisite staffing and equipment (including transport), then the eventual loss due to corruption and fraud will far exceed the supposed "savings" in not releasing funds in the first place.

Above all, the war on corruption will require more than "lip service." Government and all people in leadership positions must be seen to be openly and resolutely set against corruption. Consequently, effective sanctions/penalties must be enacted or strengthened and uncompromisingly and impartially applied as a regular feature in public management. Given adequate deterrent measures, vigorously and honestly enforced, a point will be reached beyond which even the most incorrigible person in public office will hesitate to go, realising that it is not worth taking the risk.

Agencies and Institutions Engaged in the Fight against Corruption

Currently there exist various major legislations which address corruption, namely:

The Prevention of Corruption Act 1970
The IGG Statute 1987
The Penal Code (Amendment) Statute 1987

The Penal Code
The Police Act
The Public Finance Act

While the laws may be adequate, experience has shown that prosecutions in corruption cases have been hampered by the laws of evidence, especially the accomplice rule. This rule states "that the evidence of an accomplice must be corroborated before a conviction can be based on it. In cases of corruption, both the giver and recipient are accomplices. If corrupt people are to be convicted, this rule should be changed to allow an accomplice to give credible evidence against corrupt officials or persons.

The NRM Government emphasised its determination to fight corruption in its 10-Point Programme, Article 7 of which states:

> Elimination of corruption and misuse of power: Africa being a continent that is never in shortage of problems, has also the problem of corruption—particularly bribery. Therefore, to enable the tackling of our backwardness, corruption must be eliminated once and for all.

The Inspector General of Government

To ensure that the above objectives are translated into action and to spearhead the fight against corruption and bribery, Government, in 1987, established the Office of the Inspector-General of Government (IGG), specifically required by law "to take necessary measures for the detection and prevention of corruption in public offices."

These are indeed laudable objectives. However, the fact that the IGG's reports and findings are only advisory to the President and are not published, has resulted in considerable delays and frustration in giving practical and visible effect to his efforts. The IGG Statute should therefore be amended to empower the IGG not only to investigate but also to prosecute cases of corruption. (This has been granted in the new constitution promulgated in 1995 -Ed). The Director of Public Prosecutions (DPP) will continue to deal with other cases in the Courts of Law.

Furthermore, the IGG is, by virtue of the small complement of his staff, basically confined to Kampala; and is consequently not able to regularly monitor and investigate corruption and abuse of power in other parts of the country. These problems will require to be specifically addressed to enable the IGG to discharge his heavy and laudable responsibility.

The Police Force

In 1986 when the NRM took power, the Police Force, which should be the vanguard in the war against corruption, was itself corrupt, grossly undermanned, ill-equipped, poorly housed and was, and still is, woefully underpaid. Important steps have since been taken to recruit and train a better educated police force. With the help of friendly bilateral sources more equipment and transport have been made available, and the prospects for gradual improvement are good. We deal with the general subject of the Police Force elsewhere—Chapter 19—in this report.

In the specific context of the fight against corruption, the most relevant arm of the Police, the Criminal Investigation Department (CID) is, to date, not adequately equipped or trained to effectively fight crime generally and corruption in particular. The situation is aggravated by lack of effective and strict supervision by senior officers, hence the reported corruption in the Force itself. For example, court exhibits and case files of persons accused of corruption (or other serious crimes) have at times mysteriously disappeared between the office of the DPP, the Police Stations and the Courts. Consequently the person who has embezzled millions of public funds goes completely free, thus making a mockery of the due process of law.

The Judiciary

The role of the Judiciary, as an institution engaged in the fight against corruption, is important and complex. By the very nature of the institution, the Judiciary cannot perform in isolation. Its effectiveness depends on other complementary organs, such as the Attorney-General's Department and the Police. Accordingly, the problems that hamper the Judiciary often either originate elsewhere or are compounded by other problems beyond its control.

Three such problems are relevant here. At the top of the list is the inability of Government to attract and retain the best and most experienced lawyers in the public service because of its uncompetitively low salaries and poor conditions of service. In addition, the lack of funds for various required activities—including transport and hotel accommodation, and so on—has often had the effect of placing judges, magistrates, lawyers and other judicial officers in embarrassing and potentially compromising positions, not to mention the delays in the processes of the law due to absences of prosecutors and witnesses as a result of funds not being readily available. Thirdly, there is the nature of the law itself and of the judicial rules of procedure, such as the "accomplice rule" referred to above, which sometimes allow "technicalities" to have the effect of frustrating the meting out of justice in corruption cases.

The point we wish to make here is two-fold. First, it should be realised that to the extent that members of the Judiciary face chronic problems that result in low morale and reduced efficiency, fertile ground for corruption is being created, thereby compromising their effectiveness. Second, judges and magistrates have to apply the law as it is. Consequently, where the existing laws are unsuitable for the specific crime of corruption, then appropriate amendments or even fresh legislation should be enacted to strengthen the hand of the Judiciary in combating corruption.

The Auditor-General's Office

During the turbulent past, the Auditor-General's Office made valiant efforts to audit and report on Government Accounts. But there was then no (except in 1980-85 but that was also a weak house - Ed) parliament and no active Public Accounts Committee. Consequently no effective follow-up could be instituted even after the Auditor-General had reported cases of gross corruption or embezzlement of public funds. In addition, the security of individual auditors was at stake.

Since 1986, with the revival of Parliament (NRC) and the Public Accounts Committee, the Auditor-General's Reports are now regularly written and debated. However, the major problems staff in the Auditor-General's Office face are the low staff salaries and poor conditions of service which frustrate the Auditor-General's attempts to attract and retain qualified accountants who are lured to better remunerated jobs in the private and parastatal sectors. Since timeliness of the Auditor-General's Reports is essential for prompt action on lapses and abuses bordering on corruption, it is to be hoped that the problems militating against efficiency of the Department will be attended to as top priority.

The institution of the Public Accounts Committee (PAC)

As stated above the PAC has since 1986 done a commendable job in following up cases of corruption, abuse of office and straightforward embezzlement of public funds. It is important that special attention should be given to solving some of the problems of the above institutional agencies which are crucial in the fight against corruption.

Recommendations

Concurrently with the normal efforts of the agencies discussed above, more action is required to sensitize our people, both within and outside the public service, to the dangers of corruption. We face a major problem inherent in the nature of corruption, namely: "the satisfied customer" relationship, which makes it difficult to get evidence needed to successfully prosecute offenders. Under existing laws both the giver and the receiver of a bribe are committing a crime. But if both sides are satisfied by the outcome of their deal, neither will be willing to co–operate with the prosecution should any aspect of the matter go to court. Moreover, since such transactions are quite often carried out in private or in secret, there are usually no witnesses to the act, and no "scene of the crime" to be visited by detectives.

In effect, the state will be fighting a losing battle from the start if it depends mainly on post facto acting, detecting and punishing after acts of corruption have been committed.

Here is another situation in which prevention may be better than cure. For instance, it is agreed that poor pay in the Public Service is highly conducive to corruption. Yet within the Public Service itself there exist many loopholes through which a few officials embezzle huge sums that could have gone towards better pay for all. Thus, quite apart from such measures as reducing the size of the Public Service, which we are recommending, there is need to intensify preventive anti-corruption measures.

We have already indicated the need for better or tighter controls in the Service to forestall abuse of office. Among the many financial abuses that can be prevented are the following: Many senior and middle-level staff corruptly divert large sums of money regularly, ostensibly to pay workers who turn out to be "ghost workers." The block sum release for payment of group employee wages is another weakness. It is also known that many employees manage to hold two or three jobs concurrently, each supposed to be full-time. Apparently, this practice is widespread in the teaching and medical fields, and it should be obvious that the rampant financial abuse that goes with it cannot take place without the connivance or condonement of Headmasters or District Education Officers. We also found evidence of systematic interception and diversion of funds earmarked for up-country staff salaries and allowances, leading to delays of several months before the salaries are eventually paid. Evidently, some headquarters staff divert such funds and invest them in quick turnover projects and then deceive the concerned staff that the Treasury had not yet released the money. In many cases sums are actually embezzled so that the payments, especially allowances, never finally reach the intended employees in the Districts. There is also the practice of "week-end allowance," reportedly paid to senior staff and political leaders for trips to their constituencies and home towns. All these allowances, usually paid in cash, are not properly accounted for, and nobody checks whether or not the trips were actually made and what official duties were performed to justify such use of public funds.

The overwhelming need therefore is for the Public Service first to put its house in order. It must plug the loopholes and enforce procedural controls, so as to conserve funds to enable Government to meet the cry of public servants for better pay. In the specific case of delayed payment of salaries and allowances, there are serious implications for morale where district staff are concerned. In view of the policy of decentralisation, which this Commission supports, the problem will get worse if measures are not instituted to ensure that salaries, allowances and pensions for up-country districts are transmitted promptly and that they reach the intended beneficiaries.

To overcome the particular problem of delayed salaries in the field due to diversion or embezzlement of funds, we recommend that wherever possible staff should be encouraged to open personal bank or savings accounts at their stations. The funds would then be sent direct to the bank branch for the respective salaries to be credited to individual accounts of listed workers. Since the Uganda Commercial Bank network now has a branch in each district, it should be possible to make arrangements accordingly. In so doing, Government should ensure:

a. that actual cash (not cheques) is physically made available to all branches so that the banks do not plead delayed payment due to liquidity problems;
b. that the funds are released on time to the banks before the end of each month; and
c. that, to stop unscrupulous officials using the Treasury as a scapegoat, the release date is made known - to all Districts.

Further measures

Beyond the foregoing preventive considerations specific to corruption in the Public Service, the war against corruption on the national front should be vigorously fought along the following lines:

i. *Leadership Code of Conduct*
There is urgent need for establishing and effectively enforcing a Leadership Code of Conduct for all public office holders so that both political and public servants of all grades emphasize their accountability to the nation they are supposed to serve. The Code, details of which are given in Chapter 3 of the Report, should be vigorously enforced by the institutions discussed above and the national political leadership generally, without fear or favour. There is a general belief that the Anti-Corruption Law catches only the small people while the big people go unpunished. To dispel this notion and demonstrate that Government means business when it talks against corruption, the IGG should detail a special team of his staff to resolutely investigate reports concerning senior staff and political leaders.

ii. *Screening of prospective appointees*
The National Resistance Council (NRC) (or parliament now) should establish a Committee to review backgrounds and qualifications before they clear candidates for senior public/political office. Any candidate with a questionable background concerning honesty or corruption should be disqualified. The Committee should consist of one NRC (or MO now) member from each District. However, care must be taken to ensure selection of members who will consider and decide on national rather than sectarian/ representational considerations. Such reviews should cover nominees for senior political, parastatal and diplomatic positions put forward by the President as the Appointing Authority. The candidates (appointees) should have a right to appear before the Committee to ensure that decisions/advice to the President on their suitability or otherwise are based on facts.

iii. *Enforcement of anti-corruption law*

a. Vigorous efforts should be made to strictly enforce all anti-corruption laws, rules and regulations promptly and without fear or favour. Whoever violates the anti corruption law must be brought to justice and made to suffer the appropriate penalties as laid down by the law.

b. The Public Accounts Committee should be given a small but carefully selected secretariat to assist in following up PAC queries, and in ensuring that the Police and the IGG deal promptly with cases raised by the PAC and where necessary prosecutions instituted.

c. Appropriate legislation should be enacted to protect the confidentiality, identity and safety of "whistle blowers" so that more reports about corruption would continue to be received by the Police, IGG, PAC and the proposed Petition Committees.

d. Wherever an expenditure of funds will aid in the fight against corruption, such funds should be provided as a "top priority" to avoid the "penny-wise, pound-foolish" syndrome.

e. Sufficient numbers of qualified staff should be recruited for the PAC and the Auditor-General's Office to permit timely inspection and audits of current budget financial year activities. This would enable more evidence to be assembled before it gets "lost" or destroyed. The prospect of early detection would serve as a deterrent against corrupt practices.

iv. *Establishment of anti-corruption tribunal*

Some countries have taken measures to curb corruption by passing specially stiff laws and by establishing special anti-corruption tribunals, which not being hampered by the ordinary procedural traditions and technicalities of the regular courts, would therefore deal with corruption cases more expeditiously. To ensure quick but fair trials, the National Resistance Council (or parliament now) should be asked to establish a special Anti-Corruption Tribunal, the functions of which would include the following:

a. To expeditiously try all corruption cases emanating from the Police Force (CID), the Inspector-General of Government, or from proceedings of the Public Accounts Committee (PAC) and to pass sentences without undue delay.

b. To impose heavy penalties (provided by laws to be enacted by Parliament which would be commensurate with the seriousness of the crime. For people, both senior and junior, who are in fiduciary positions, especially stiff and exemplary penalties should be imposed to deter others from engaging in corrupt practices. For example, for each UShs 100,000 embezzled or goods of equivalent value, the convict should be given a one-year mandatory jail sentence.

Composition

The Tribunal's composition should comprise respected members of the public and elected representatives of the people. The system should operate at two levels: the Tribunal at the national level and the Petition Committees at District levels, as below:

I. National Anti-Corruption Tribunal
The Tribunal would consist of:
Chairman: An experienced and respected person who may or may not be a lawyer
Member: A serving senior officer not below the rank of a Permanent Secretary
Member: A Senior Army Officer not below the rank of a Lieutenant Colonel
Member: A Senior Police Officer not below the rank of a Senior Assistant Commissioner
Two NRC members elected by NRC (or MPs now - Ed)
One legal advisor appointed by the Attorney-General/Solicitor General

II. District Petition Committees
The District Petition Committee would consist of:
Chairman: Elected by RC V (now LCV)
Vice-Chairman: District Executive Director
One Representative from each County
District Treasurer
District Finance Officer
District Police Commander

Personnel Officer: Secretary

The function of the Committee will be specifically to receive reports on corruption, maladministration, abuse of office, gross inefficiency, rudeness by public employees, or straightforward embezzlement of Government or public property. The Committee should be easily accessible and should accept verbal as well as written reports. The District Petition Committees would have power to deal with petitions and complaints from members of the public in their Districts, but graver cases requiring countrywide investigations and heavier penalties would be referred to the IGG or the Police with a report on the Committee's findings and recommendations for prosecution before the National Tribunal. The District Petition Committees would also function as a simplified District Ombudsman to ensure greater efficiency and to curb misuse of power before it is too late. It is important that both the RCs (now LCs) and the public service should participate in petition committees to ensure that fair and quick investigations and decisions are made on petitions.

We would also recommend that as an encouragement, Government should seriously consider introducing an incentive scheme in the form of a commission to be paid to staff of any agencies or institutions engaged in the fight against corruption. The commission would be based on a percentage of the moneys saved or recovered as a result of their investigations or actions. Receivers of such commissions would also include "whistle blowers" or other people who give information leading to a successful recovery of embezzled public funds.

Penalties to be imposed on convicted persons

Finally, corruption is a serious crime; therefore the punishment must be made to fit the crime. The Anti-Corruption Law (1970) and the Penal Codes should be appropriately amended to provide for the following:

i. All embezzled monies should be returned to the state and misappropriated properties or goods should be forfeited.
ii. Mandatory minimum sentences should be prescribed for each count.
iii. All properties belonging to the convicted person, even when conveniently registered in the names of other people, should be traced and forfeited.
iv. Funds in foreign bank accounts of convicted persons and their properties abroad should, if not properly accounted for, be attached and retrieved with the assistance of the governments of the countries concerned.
v. Persons convicted of corruption should be disqualified for life from holding public office.

vi. In cases of public servants charged with corruption or embezzlement but who get acquitted for lack of evidence or other technicalities, Government as employer should exercise its right to dispense with the services of such staff, the court acquittal notwithstanding, if it has reasonable cause, from the circumstances of the case, to doubt their honesty, integrity or good faith.

5 Ethics, Accountability and Transparency in Uganda, An Assessment

Petter Langseth and *Jeremy Pope*

Introduction

An Economic Development Institute Regulatory Reform and Private Enterprise Division and Transparency International (TI) mission visited Uganda at the invitation of the Government of the Republic of Uganda, extended by the Inspector General of Government (IGG), Mr Augustine Ruzindana. It was present in the country from 7 to 17 December, 1994. The combined mission comprised Petter Langseth, Katrina Sharkey (ED); Jeremy Pope (Managing Director, Transparency International, Berlin); Laurence Cockcroft (Director, Transparency International); Joe Githong (Director, Transparency International); and Peter Gisle (Consultant).

This report touches on aspects of wide-ranging public sector reform from the point of view of the containment of corruption.

A number of formal and informal meetings were held. While we were in Uganda, in addition to our formal programme of meetings with relevant actors, we also attended two major conferences. Both meetings brought together a significant number of Ugandans who were well placed to brief us on aspects of the present situation.

The first was the Workshop on Designing a Programme to Enhance Ethics, Transparency and Accountability in Uganda, held at the Colline Hotel near Kampala on 9 and 10 December 1994, organised by the Office of the IGG. This was a particularly significant event, and we return to discuss its achievements later in our report.

The second was the Conference on Corruption, Democracy and Human Rights in East and Central Africa, held at the Lake Victoria Hotel, Entebbe, Uganda, from 12–14 December, 1994. This was organised by the Africa Leadership Forum in collaboration with TI and supported by the European Commission. This, too, carried forward a consensus for action.

Summary findings

The mission approached its task with a deep awareness of the turbulent and destructive fifteen years which had so blighted Uganda's history. Despite such a legacy, the country is rapidly recovering. The currency is now convertible, inflation has been largely brought under control and flight capital is returning to the country. The transformation of the political environment, too, into one of freedom and absence of repression is admirable. In civil society a critical academic and a very outspoken (if at times irresponsible) press is generally at a healthy level of open debate. A largely elected Constituent Assembly conducted a well-publicised debate on a new draft Constitution (prepared by a Commission which consulted widely across the country in the course of its work) culminating in the promulgation of the 1995 Constitution. The public administration is also rapidly regrouping; a wide-ranging programme of civil service reform is being put into place; civil service numbers are being reduced from 320,000 to about 150,000 (the present size is 169,000); and independent and reinforced structures are now investigating books, accounts and events without (it would seem) excessive interference. Included in the reform programme is also a divestiture (privatisation) exercise.

Nevertheless, the country continues to face problems and particularly corruption which is still widespread in Uganda both at the bottom and at the top. Corruption is primarily a means of survival on the part of junior civil servants and others; at the top, it involves the spoilage and misapplication (even misappropriation) of funds on a large scale by senior civil servants and politicians. Corruption is thus constituting a threat to the country's democratic and economic recovery, to its ability to attract direct foreign investment, and to sustain present levels of donor support.

Combating corruption therefore looms large among the government's preoccupations and is considered by the President to be a matter of highest priority. It looms large, too, in the consciousness of the people. It is, however, also a fact that Uganda has taken more substantive and determined measures than most other countries to deal with the problem of corruption. A number of corrupt politicians—and civil servants—have been removed from office and the IGG has, under the 1995 Constitution, been given a free hand to investigate corrupt practices.

As a matter of introduction, it must, however, also be said that the population seems to continue to be unconvinced of the determination of the leadership to effectively combat corruption. Two causes are particularly given: the need for the President to balance the fight against corruption with the need to maintain national unity and heal wounds on the one hand; and the absence of formal convictions of individuals who demonstrably have plundered public funds.

The main conclusion of the mission was that the efforts of the Government are remarkable and admirable but that the effort might yet stumble unless a determined—and urgent—effort is made to rid the judiciary of corruption.

The overriding conclusion of the mission is, however, that TI should provide what assistance the Government might require to carry out its ambitious effort to fight corruption.

The Government

The impressions gained from the numerous meetings with government officials, both in the course of interviews and of the two workshops, was that corruption continues to be a major concern. Many people we met—even from the public sector—did not hesitate to classify corruption as rampant.

Corruption is a major issue in Uganda, at all levels of society. Many politicians and senior civil servants practise corruption at different levels of intensity. The ongoing privatisation process is perceived as affected by irregularities, and national and international tendering procedures are consistently perceived as prone to corruption. The civil service is perceived as corrupt.

The political process is open to vote-buying at all levels. We heard several accounts of vote-buying and suggestions that this was widespread in the context of the elections for the Constituent Assembly. Vote-buying is, of course, expensive and we heard of candidates spending many millions of shillings which they simply could not afford and did not have, in the quest for political office. Some failed and have been left with debts they can never hope to service. Others won, and presumably are now faced with making good the promises they made to their backers.

The Government of Uganda is deeply conscious of the need to combat corruption. The President himself uses every opportunity to drive the anti-corruption message home. While we were in the country he opened the rehabilitated international terminal at Entebbe Airport. Press coverage of his speech, in which he severely criticised customs and immigration officials for their corruption, was extensive.

The President has also systematically removed corrupt politicians from senior positions in the government, through a series of reshuffles. This effort is, however, apparently being hampered by the perceived necessity to give priority to the unity of the country, the implication being that this process necessitates the maintenance of certain individuals who play important roles in national political life and who would be a greater threat to political stability and national unity if they were outside the government.

The Office of the IGG

At the institutional level the centrepiece of the government's anti–corruption strategy is the Office of the IGG. This office was established some seven years ago, as a public office, with the holder directly responsible to the President. Under the 1995 Constitution the IGG is responsible to the Parliament.

The office is akin to an Ombudsman, but one whose remit is so broad as to challenge even the most bold-hearted. Charged with the general duty of protecting and promoting human rights and the rule of law in Uganda, and fostering the elimination of corruption and abuse of public office, the IGG has also specific functions to inquire into violations of human rights (including the denial of a fair trial), the methods by which law enforcement agents and the state security agencies execute their functions and interfere with the rule of law in Uganda. He also takes necessary measures to detect and prevent corruption in public office (in particular examining practices and procedures, disseminating information on the evil and dangerous effects of corruption on society and enlisting public support as well as receiving and investigating complaints of alleged or suspected corrupt practices and injustices and making recommendations for appropriate action therein). In addition, the IGG investigates the conduct of any public officer which may be connected with, or conducive to, the abuse of authority, the neglect of official duties and economic malpractice. As well as receiving complaints from the public, the IGG may initiate investigations of his own choosing.

Public Sector Reform

Corruption in Uganda, as elsewhere in Africa, is however not only an issue for the powerful or a matter of uncontrolled greed. Civil service remuneration and conditions of service have continuously deteriorated over many years in the wake of structural adjustment processes and programmes. In spite of high levels of inflation most salaries have been adjusted for many a year but still they do not permit many civil servants to survive on one salary alone. At the lowest levels we were told that some civil servants were paid 28,000 shillings a month (about $28), a small fraction of what the government estimates to be a minimum living wage.

An inevitable consequence of the need to generate additional income is that some civil servants have entered into business, some with perhaps only one customer – the department which employs them. This is neither consistent with the Standing Orders (which we are told are seldom available or enforced) nor with any concept of efficient and honest government.

We heard of people with as many as four or five jobs, as well as a need to garden for family food. Absenteeism from work appeared to be a major problem. A positive factor is that these other activities, outside the public service, have positioned a large number of those affected by the redundancies to be able to adapt reasonably quickly to their new situations.

Contrary to most other countries in Africa, Uganda has taken decisive steps to reform the public sector within the framework of a reform programme which has its genesis in the work of a comprehensive Public Sector Review Commission.

The work, which has been going on for some seven years, with considerable donor support (from Germany, United Kingdom, U.S., United Nations Development Programme, World Bank and so on) has hitherto yielded a dramatic reduction of the public service from 320,000 to about 169,000. The ultimate goal is 135,000, which should be reached shortly. (This exercise also identified some 42,000 "ghosts" – civil servants who had retired or died over the years or who never existed – on the public payroll. This figure is fairly consistent with the experiences of several other African governments.)

The next steps of the reform process include the introduction of better remuneration, including the concept of a minimum "living wage" and a reasonably coherent strategy to combat corruption, under the leadership of a committee which is expected to be chaired by the IGG.

At the end of the reform process, the government should be left with a slimmer, more efficient and much better remunerated civil service; hopefully one in which there are career prospects so that it will also be more productive and focused on key areas of governmental responsibility. But the country is at present deeply impoverished despite the inward investment which is encouraging development.

Effects of Government Actions

Considerable attention has been and is being given to strengthening the government's monitoring and enforcement agencies. Furthermore, senior officials feel that the fight against corruption in Uganda is having both a direct and an indirect impact. Senior civil servants are being removed from positions of real power and some are even being suspended, at least pending the outcome of inquiries. Furthermore, it was perceived that many individuals were being increasingly cautious and even refraining from actively pursuing corrupt activities as the risk of exposure and punishment increased.

On the other hand, we also concluded that the public generally was neither convinced that the government's efforts were serious, nor that politicians were interested in clean government. In fact, we do not think that the public was very clear on what corruption is.

Despite the government being equipped with the necessary legal and administrative frameworks and those being bolstered by the office of the IGG, senior figures in and out of government acknowledge that despite all these efforts, the perception, both among the enforcement agencies and among the wider public, is that corruption is as rampant as ever.

Public perceptions

General

All interviews with members of the civil society yielded one and the same view, albeit with differing emphasis and nuances: Government may be taking steps to fight corruption but not effectively enough. People argued that far too little was happening, too few were being successfully prosecuted and too many notoriously corrupt individuals were retaining high level positions in government.

We were also given to understand that the scepticism was largely shared by a wider public which appears to hold a cynical view of politics. Some feel, for instance, that the Constituent Assembly was taking an inordinately long time to deliberate on the new Constitution simply because members wished to draw out the proceedings in order to maximise their generous daily allowances. That people hold such a negative view of the bulk of those who must be assumed to be likely to form the elected parliament, is cause for concern.

This negative view of politicians was further highlighted by reactions to the debate which was taking place during our visit concerning the provisions of the Leadership Code. The general public clearly interpreted the debate as further evidence that most politicians had something to hide.[2]

The Press

The Ugandan press, which is being given free rein by the government, is giving the issue of corruption much prominence.

Although the press is perceived as a powerful weapon in the fight against corruption, its lack of professionalism in Uganda is clearly undermining its usefulness. The lack of professionalism is further exacerbated by the difficult financial situation of many newspapers, which make their editors vulnerable to bribery. The result is that it is difficult to distinguish investigative reporting from paid-for slander.

The Judiciary

Interviews with members of the civil society and the civil service invariably gave a rather sombre view of the judiciary. As in many other countries visited by EDI and TI, it would appear that a combination of low salaries and large differences in incomes have contributed to undermining the objectivity and the ethics of many members of the legal profession.

In many of our conversations a pattern emerged of magistrates arriving either late or not at all; of some taking bribes, both to grant bail where a defendant absconds and to give judgement; of court staff losing files and gerrymandering the allocation of magistrates at the behest of lawyers who pay them for the service they rendered; and even of witnesses and complainants being held to ransom by police who demand money to pay for the "transportation" to court of a prisoner due for trial. Witnesses become dispirited, and eventually abandon all hope of ever giving evidence and do not bother to turn up. A proposal to introduce "non-bailable offences" has been mooted, within government, but there are valid human rights and due process objections to this concept unless some provision for review is provided for deserving cases, and it is rightly one that should be examined very carefully.

We asked why the Prevention of Corruption Act 1970, with its reversal of the burden of proof where an accused was in possession of unexplained wealth out of line with his or her own income, had not been used more frequently. The answer was that judges required more than simply the possession of wealth before they would invoke the reversal of the onus of proof, such as evidence that the accused had held a position in the public sector from which he or she would have been able to profit corruptly.

In addition to their machinations with the court system, lawyers were said to bribe each other to bring about a desired settlement. It would seem from this that the defence of "only doing what was necessary to make the wheels of a corrupt machine turn" is not open to a significant number of them. The legal profession in itself has become a part of the problem. We make proposals below as to how both the judiciary and the practising profession might be encouraged to improve their performance.

Privatisation

The impact of privatisation has yet to be felt. The target for divestitures during 1993–1994 was not met; in theory, eight significant parastatal companies were to be privatised by mid–1995 (including those which should have been privatised by mid–1994). We heard informed criticism to the effect that such privatisation of parastatal companies as has already taken place has not led to the most appropriate selection of purchasers.

While privatisation seems to have been welcomed by many, the way in which it is being carried out is attracting strong criticism from those who have to deal with it. There is apprehension that the process lacks integrity, and that some senior public figures are among its beneficiaries. Nevertheless, traditional areas for corrupt activity are being removed from the private sector and the public domain for those who would be corrupt is shrinking steadily.

Public Procurement

Public procurement is, not surprisingly, a major area of fraud and corruption. We were even given the very specific information that the going rate on parastatal contracts was 8 percent. The payments go to the project managers for distribution to those who participate in the proceeds.

On the other hand, few seemed to feel that "grand corruption" in the context of international tenders was a major problem in Uganda, although there were clearly instances of such corruption.

Observations

Uganda is, unquestionably, making remarkable and apparently fairly successful efforts to fight corruption. We accept that this process has to be slow and deliberate, particularly in view of the country's turbulent past. We have been duly impressed by the gradual removal of corrupt individuals and the freedom given to the press.

We are, however, concerned that the authorities may be too cautious and that, as a consequence, they are not getting public credit for their achievements. On the contrary, a perception that the government is not doing much is widely held. This perception persists in spite of actions taken to suspend and investigate some relatively senior public servants and the dismissal from cabinet of a number of ministers. It persists, too, in spite of wide admiration for the President.

A major issue as regards the credibility of the government is, as mentioned elsewhere, the apparent absence of visible convictions of individuals who are demonstrably corrupt, and who have been found to be so by the legal system. This was also discussed at the workshop referred to above and we can but emphasize the importance of a legal process which has the full confidence of the people.

The IGG

Given the fact that the IGG's remit is much wider and deeper than that of the traditional office of the Ombudsman it is indeed remarkable that the IGG should have placed his office, over-extended though it may be, so clearly on the public, the political and administrative map despite the obvious constraints imposed by somewhat scarce resources.

On the other hand, the IGG has also been criticised for ineffectiveness and we believe that is why the 1995 Constitution has given his office more "teeth." The IGG has, in addition to other arms of government, been empowered to investigate and prosecute corruption. This should help the office of the IGG to overcome the difficulties which have hitherto limited its capacity to apprehend the offenders and, if found guilty, punish them.

However, despite the constitutional empowerment of the IGG the public is not yet convinced the beneficiaries of corruption have been brought to book.

Public Awareness

Our major concern is the population at large which seems to be largely resigned to the fact that those holding power are corrupt. Although we understand – and indeed saw that many do complain through the press and elsewhere – it appears clear that the vast majority do not.

We believe that it is imperative for the government to incorporate the population in any fight against corruption. A strictly administrative campaign against corruption is not only lopsided since it implies the exclusion of those from which funds are being stolen, but the exclusion of the general public also implies the renunciation of the most powerful monitoring system available, that of the consumer and the voters.

We consequently believe that the government should seriously consider launching a major campaign to fight corruption. This notion is consistent with the recommendations of the workshop referred to above and should be given high priority.

A campaign of this kind should exploit all available means, from information pamphlets and posters, films and radio programmes through the theatre, telephone complaint "hot-lines" and competitions of all description. All available resources, too, should be mobilised, including civil society, professional and service groups and those with moral authority in the area of religion. It goes without saying that the campaigns should be in the vernacular as well as in English.

The focal points for the campaign might be that:

- the public have a right to certain public services without further payment;
- they should resist and report any demands for such illicit payments;
- there are complaint mechanisms available, what these are and how they should be used;
- those who enrich themselves at public expense are stealing "their" money, and should be objects of contempt and derision, not role models;

> neither grand corruption nor petty extortion form any part of "African culture." Rather, the abuse of public office by corrupt officials has served to diminish, to some extent, traditions of hospitality and generosity.[3]

The campaign would be most effective were it to have the open and active support of the President himself.

Procurement

As elsewhere, public procurement, be it national or international, is a major source of corruption in Uganda.

There are two separate aspects to the international dimension to corruption in Uganda: the first, a willingness on the part of overseas suppliers to offer (they might say to have to offer) bribes to obtain business, and the second, an inability on the part of the enforcement authorities to retrieve from abroad the proceeds of "grand corruption" where these have been secreted abroad.

We believe that the government should consider adopting a "no bribery pledge" approach similar to the one being used on a trial basis in Ecuador and overhaul its procurement systems by involving the private sector more actively in its design and implementation.

Breakdown of the Rule of Law

In most countries a collapse of the rule of law would suggest a lawless anarchy. Such is certainly not the case in Uganda. That it is not says much for the tolerance and long-suffering nature of most Ugandans.

Compounding the problems of enforcement in corruption cases is a judicial administration which most categorise as thoroughly corrupt, not just in handling major fraud and corruption cases but in their daily work. Of course, there are outstanding exceptions, but at the magistrates' court level, the police, the prosecutors, the court staff and most of the magistrates are regarded with contempt.

The ethics of the legal profession also seem to be strongly questioned, not least by practitioners themselves. One former practitioner now in government described his former colleagues as being even worse than the courts. This, too, must obviously be a matter of great concern.

The Fight Against Corruption

We can, of course, but surmise as to the impact which the steps taken to expose corruption may have had on its incidence. Our observations are necessarily no more than impressions, and they are only offered with the realisation that others better placed to comment may well disagree.

Secrecy is, of course, the hallmark of the corrupt, at least at the level of grand corruption, and so despite claims that much petty corruption (and even some significant corruption) takes place in the open, it is in any country difficult to measure the progress made in containing corruption, especially in the short term. Not without some caution, we would imagine that – despite the overwhelming and near universal public view that anything goes and that no shame is attached when the corrupt are caught and exposed – the considerable publicity given to the reports made by the IGG and those of the Auditor General must have acted as a deterrent to some, even if the official disclosures have apparently not shocked the public consciousness to the extent that the enforcement community must have hoped. Perhaps, as some suggested, these achievements in deterrence have to some extent been obscured by an unruly press.

When we looked at the government's total strategy, it appears to be one designed to break the psychology of corruption, and to do this steadily by a series of actions—a strengthening of key institutions throughout the civil service (including training but in particular by carefully-targeted enhanced pay for those holding critical positions, including pay supplements from donors), privatisation, publicity and action against some. Gradually, it seems, the message is starting to get through to the corrupt that the rules of the game are changing, and that they should change with it. The strategy is, however, a sophisticated one and yields few obvious sacrificial lambs. The message may be getting through to the corrupt, but it now needs to get through to the general public.

The Vice President was among those who expressed the view that in a situation of rampant and systemic corruption, to clamp down on the most junior staff when wages were beneath a pittance would be to compound injustices; and that to select and make examples of those higher up would create areas of extreme ill-will as family groups demanded explanations as to why their particular brothers or sisters had been singled out for such treatment.

We believe that the sum total of all these efforts must have contributed to a reduction in corruption levels by reason of an increasing perception of the likelihood of detection and humiliation. Be that as it may, in the view of the general public the very real achievements we have mentioned seem to be seen as being little more than a show, as a play to the gallery.

With the pending introduction of new salary scales for the civil service, the government is presented with a unique opportunity to reintroduce the concept of members of the civil service being servants of the general public and that the population need no longer– and must no longer – tolerate corrupt practices and inferior services by officials at any level.

It is, we feel, important that these messages come across as a package. As a consequence, public servants should get the message that they now have a job they may not wish to risk, and that they stand to lose it should they act corruptly. The public will get the message that they now have an adequately remunerated public service and must not tolerate further corruption.

Part Three

INSTITUTIONAL MECHANISMS

6 Combating Corruption in Uganda

Augustine Ruzindana

Introduction

Corruption used to be associated primarily with societies and regimes in Africa, Latin America, Asia and other underdeveloped regions. But, with the exposure of the pervasive rottenness of the Italian business and political leadership; the frequent revelations in parliament and the press of the malpractices of the Japanese leaders; the recent exposure, trial and conviction of senior ministers in France; the discovery of the lavish expenditures by managers of public enterprises like Ala Atali, former adviser to President Mitterand, and subsequently head of a European bank charged with the reconstruction of Russia and Eastern Europe; and the grumbling in Europe about lack of accountability at the EEC headquarters in Brussels, there is clear evidence that corruption is not restricted to developing countries.

So far there are no international mechanisms to control and monitor the phenomenon of corruption except the new initiative of Transparency International. Interest in corruption that is beginning to be shown by the World Bank and other multilateral institutions is timely and will attract due emphasis in understanding and combating it.

After gaining independence in 1962, Uganda had a very promising future. The three great enemies of development – poverty, ignorance and disease – were targeted for elimination. Since that time, however, these enemies have increased, and corruption and repression can be added to the list. Unfortunately, corruption complicates the situation because it is an obstacle to the struggle against the other enemies. It creates an impediment to economic progress because it interferes with production and distribution of goods and services at all levels in all sectors of the economy. It is also an impediment to democracy because it subverts the democratic process of elections, of government administration, law enforcement and the legal process. It results in moral decay and perverted social values. It saps the social fabric of a nation, paving the way to corruption as an inevitable way of life. "Man eateth where he worketh" then becomes the accepted rationalisation of corruption.

Since independence and the ensuing political upheavals in Uganda, job insecurity became a major cause of corruption. Senior public servants had to hurriedly maximise their earnings while in office since they were not sure of the length of their stay in office. The "ten percent" commission became institutionalised as a result of this insecurity.

The post-Amin period saw three governments in one year, and the rate of corruption reached its highest level. The period was characterised by outright plunder, huge commissions, bribes and embezzlement. Within a few weeks of holding office, many officials accumulated a substantial amount of money which was stashed away abroad, or invested in foreign properties. In Uganda, and I daresay in Africa in general, the fact that those in power hold transitory positions contributes a great deal to the occurrence of corruption. There is a great deal of insecurity at the individual and systemic levels. This leads those in public offices to loot whatever and whenever they can so that when the inevitable termination occurs, they have some accumulated "savings" with which to cushion their lives.

This feeling of insecurity of public officials has been exacerbated by structural policies that lead to retrenchment and layoffs from the public service. Every now and then, the relevant minister announces a reduction in the number of civil servants or soldiers, and since those to leave are not identified, everyone feels the need to "save" for the expected layoff: the level of corruption is therefore increased. Government policies and pronouncements are sometimes themselves the causes of corruption because they tend to accentuate the level of insecurity among public employees.

In Uganda, we have faced the problem of an expanding population with a diminishing economy. Upon independence, the people were relatively well-off. But thirty-two years later, with three times the population, a reduced economy cannot support the populace even at the level at which they were thirty-two years ago. As a result, strong pressure is exerted on public officials to use their influence to "fix" their relatives and friends in employment, very often in positions for which they are not qualified. This is what is called nepotism. It is nurtured by traditional expectation that a person who happens to occupy a position of influence must use that influence for the benefit of his people.

In Africa, virtually every change of government, whether violent or peaceful, is justified on the basis of removing corrupt governments. Inquiry commissions or tribunals with extensive summary powers are then set up to combat corruption. Yet the problem persists and seems to defy all measures put in place against it. We may, therefore, be tempted to conclude that the correct diagnosis of the problem has yet to be made, or that the correct methods to deal with corruption have yet to be found, or that maybe only half-hearted measures have been taken against it. Another possible conclusion could be that the standards, values and demands of post-industrial societies are being unrealistically imposed on societies whose standards and values are still largely those of pre-industrial societies. It is imperative, therefore, that we find the right diagnosis of the problem and the correct solutions.

Forms/Types of Corruption Found in Uganda

In December 1989, the UNO (Crime Prevention and Criminal Justice Department) organised a seminar on corruption in government in The Hague. This seminar was attended by twenty developing and nine developed countries, and a number of non-governmental organisations. It was at this seminar that I learned a great deal about the phenomenon of corruption, particularly in other African countries. Not surprisingly, the different types of corruption, the causes and the effects are generally the same. Corruption can take many forms, ranging from the trivial to the monumental. It can include the misuse of simple procedures, or of policy instruments (for example, tariffs and credit, the enforcement of laws and rules, or the observance of contract regulations). It can occur in the private or public sector, or both simultaneously. Corruption can involve threats, promises or both; it can be initiated by a public official or by a member of the public; it can entail acts of omission or commission; it can be inside or outside an organisation.

The types of corruption found in Uganda which I will mention below are also found in other African countries. We have identified the following:

- bribery, extortion
- illegal use of public assets for private gain
- over-invoicing and under-invoicing
- payment of salaries and wages to non-existent workers ("ghost workers")

- payment for goods not supplied or services not rendered ("air supply")
- undercharging of taxes and duties on exports and imports involving false classifications
- false declarations and false tariffs; purchases of goods and services at inflated prices
- "ten percent commissions"
- fraud and embezzlement
- improper payments
- misappropriation of public assets
- court decisions in which awards for damages of very large sums of money do not correspond to the injury actually suffered, or the indefinite number of adjournments of hearing of cases or of given judgements
- the removal of documents from case files or even the disappearance of whole files

Nepotism and patronage, sometimes called tribalism or sectarianism, are also forms of corruption. Neglect or negligence of duty could also be called corruption since one is paid for work not done.

The experience of Africa may actually enlarge or widen the understanding of corruption as many cases handled as corruption cases in Africa may not be considered as such in the developed countries, or in fact may not occur at all. Conversely, types of corruption which are considered important in the developed countries may not be significant in Africa (for example, money laundering, drug trafficking, and organised crime are not yet significant in Africa). Corruption in Africa is mainly a problem of the ethical standards of public officials and the parties (transnational corporations, local business people and members of the public) with whom they come in contact. It is, therefore, not enough to investigate the activities of public officials and leave out the other parties, yet this is often the case.

The forms of corruption mentioned above may have different causes, but the conditions that provide a conducive environment for corruption are often weak systems which lack the necessary institutionalised control mechanisms or, if systems exist, then a wholesale breakdown of these systems is the main cause. Where systems have broken down, the first control to suffer is accountability. Eventually, a feeling of immunity characterises the system so that politicians and civil servants think themselves and their actions immune to any challenges against them.

Effects of Corruption

We in the under-developed world should actually be more concerned about corruption because its effects are more harmful to us than they are to the developed countries. It is true that corruption exists in the developed countries as well, but it does not obstruct the normal functioning of the social system of those countries. In Africa, corruption has hampered national, social and economic progress and, to some extent, even political progress has been impaired. Corruption involves the transfer of public resources, services and assets from public to private use. The diversion sometimes entails transferring funds to foreign countries, thereby causing harmful effects to economic development.

Coupled with outright economic and political mismanagement, it has led to political instability and gross abuse of power. Corruption has led to bad roads, poor medical services, poor schools, and falling educational standards. It is also responsible for the disappearance of whole projects which have been funded; the delayed completion of projects; the disappearance of foreign aid; an insufficient amount of imported goods than was paid for; the reduction and ruin of national assets; a reduction of production capacity in industry, agriculture, services, and so on; the incomplete repair of buildings, equipment, vehicles, roads and so forth that was paid for; the undelivered goods and services which have been paid for many times over; and the requirement of "ten percent commissions" in order to receive tender or contract awards. All this results in poor terms and conditions of service for all workers.

The sum total of all these accumulated losses in every area of public expenditure is colossal economic destruction. The majority of the population is adversely affected by corruption. Therefore, if Africa is to realise progress at a faster pace, corruption must be curbed or eliminated altogether.

Corruption impairs not only political and economic development, but also administrative effectiveness and efficiency. It undermines the legitimacy of political leaders and political institutions, and thus government is less able to rely on the co-operation and support of the public. As a result, government is forced to resort to force and coercive measures in order to maintain public order. The resulting political instability and social unrest hinders development and may lead to violent government change.

Corruption also leads to economic waste and inefficiency because of its effects on the allocation of funds, on production and on consumption. Gains obtained from corruption are unlikely to be transferred to the investment sector since ill-gotten money is either used in conspicuous consumption, or is transferred to foreign bank accounts. Such transfers represent a leakage from the domestic economy. Corruption results in allocation inefficiency as it may permit the least efficient contractor to bribe his way to government contracts. Since the cost of bribes is included in the price of goods supplied and services rendered, there is always an in-built overpricing mechanism, which means that the consumer does not get value for money. Corruption also distorts the laws of supply and demand and leads to the misallocation of resources. Its gains tend to direct labour from productive non-corrupt activities to areas where corruption is possible. Since it affects recruitment and promotion patterns, the people with the best potential may not be recruited at all, and allocation of positions may be inefficient. It directs employees' energies away from socially valuable activities towards less valuable activities.

Corruption generates administrative inefficiency and ineffectiveness by creating an atmosphere of distrust through all levels of public administration. As a result, delegation of authority is hindered and productivity in administration is reduced. Patronage and nepotism tend to lead to the recruitment of inept and incompetent individuals. It leads to frustration of professionally competent and honest civil servants. It subverts trust, inhibits innovation, and intimidates and subdues honest officials into silence.

Measures against corruption

In Africa corruption is handled differently in different countries. Some countries have taken the absurd position that corruption does not exist there. But in Uganda, we acknowledge corruption to be a major problem and a number of mechanisms to combat it have been implemented—one of them being the creation of the Office of the Inspector General of Government (IGG).

The IGG office was formed in September 1986 to investigate, among other things, corruption on a permanent basis. The functions of the office with regard to corruption are outlined in the Inspector General of Government Statute, No. 2 of 1988, as follows:

Section 7(1) of the Statute says that the IGG is charged with the duty of "eliminating and fostering the elimination of corruption and abuse of public offices."

Section 7(1) (c) of the Statute requires the IGG to take necessary measures for the detection and prevention of corruption in public offices and in particular:

i. to examine the practices and procedures of the said offices in order to facilitate the discovery of corrupt practices and to secure the revision of methods of work or procedures which, in the opinion of the Inspector General of Government, may be conducive to corrupt practices;

ii. to advise the said offices on ways and means of preventing corrupt practices, and on methods of work or procedures conducive to the effective performance of their duties and which, in the opinion of the Inspector General of Government, would reduce the incidence of corruption;

iii. to disseminate information on the evil and dangerous effects of corruption on society;

iv. to enlist and foster public support against corrupt practices; and

v. to receive and investigate complaints of alleged or suspected corrupt practices and injustices, and make recommendations for appropriate action thereon;

(d) to investigate the conduct of any public officer which may be connected with or conductive to:

i the abuse of his office or authority;

ii. the neglect of his official duties;

iii. economic malpractice by the officer."

The IGG office has been incorporated in the 1995 Constitution with more powers of investigation and prosecution than those under the above-mentioned. Moreover, the IGG is now responsible to Parliament rather than to the President.

Besides the IGG, there is the Prevention of Corruption Act, 1970 which confers on the Director of Public Prosecutions powers of search, seizure, arrest and interrogation of people suspected of corruption, in conjunction with the police. The Penal Code also provides for the different corruption offences like fraud, embezzlement, false accounting and abuse of office. Though this law was enacted in 1970, until the NRM took office it generally remained idle.

The Public Accounts Committee (PAC), which is a Standing Committee of Parliament, like the Auditor General's office which is supposed to submit reports to it, had all gone into a long slumber. They are now very active again. Accounting officers are occasionally called upon to appear before the Auditor General and PAC to account for the public funds entrusted to them to manage.

The other essential measure which has been put in place is the Leadership Code. In all countries, there is a leadership code, whether written or unwritten. This is because corruption can only exist with the connivance, even if passive, of the political leadership and the public. Therefore, it can only be eradicated when both the political leadership and the public make a concerted effort not to tolerate it any more. The leadership code is one of the means of binding leaders to behave themselves. Leadership codes serve the purpose of committing leaders not to be corrupt and they also help the public not to tolerate it when corruption occurs.

The Leadership Code in existence in Uganda provides for the annual declaration of income, assets and liabilities by leaders. It gives a minimum standard of behaviour and conduct for leaders with regard to gifts and benefits in kind, and with regard to conflict of interest, contracts and tenders in which a leader may have an interest, and with regard to the use or abuse of public property. The code also gives the legal sanctions that may be taken against a leader who violates the provisions of the code. Like the office of the IGG the leadership has been enshrined in the 1995 Constitution. However, this code has not yet served as a strong check against corruption because its implementation has been slow but public pressure is mounting to have it vigorously enforced. Efforts are underway to extend its scope to include spouses and children and to make the declaration of assets and liabilities public.

The most important measure taking place, however, is the democratisation process. The NRM government came into power in January 1986 with a democratisation programme. There is now freedom of the press and, as a result, corruption is vigorously being exposed in public meetings, and in memoranda addressed to the IGG and other offices.

Accountability and transparency within public administration is gradually being established even though corruption persists as a major problem.

In the long run, the best way to prevent corruption is by opening government business to public control. The basic element of control implicit in democratic government is the responsibility of government to the people. The greater the involvement of the people in public affairs, the more the control exerted on government.

Though a leader in a non-democratic system may be personally honest and even though in a democracy there may be a lot of corrupt officials, democracy in general checks corruption in government. Corruption, which amounts to abuse of office and betrayal of public trust, also undermines political stability since it brings the leadership of the country into disrepute. A leader who is not respected loses public confidence and mandate. A corrupt government is worse than no government at all because it abuses the very nature and purpose of government and the rights of the people. This is why for Uganda the fight against corruption is an important component of the democratisation process.

Examples of cases handled by the office of the IGG

Misdeclaration of goods contrary to the Uganda Customs and Excise Act

This was a case in which a local company was importing goods under the cover of a European religious non-governmental organisation (NGO), which was exempted from import duties and taxes because of its charitable and relief activities. The office of the IGG investigated and had the director of the company arrested by the police for evasion of import duties and taxes. However, instead of charging him in court, the short cut of having him pay all the duties and taxes due before being released from police custody was taken. The NGO also sacked a number of its employees who were involved in the racket but they were not charged in court. The actual guilty party, the principal European contact in the NGO who doubled as the director of the private company, was never affected because not enough evidence was assembled against him.

Fictitious Workshop of the Kagera Basin Organisation

Funds were requisitioned in a Ministry for the purpose of funding a workshop to take place in a southern border town in Uganda. Investigations revealed that no workshop ever took place, and none was ever proposed, planned or discussed in the particular Ministry. The officer whose authority was used to requisition for the funds never signed the relevant documents, and it was clear that his signature was forged because he was not present in the Ministry at that time. This is a clear case where payment for a fictitious purpose was possible because of weak controls and weak accountability—no one had asked questions until our investigations took place.

Payment for repair of 50 Kilometres of road that was never done

A company was awarded a contract "to repair potholes and edge failure with hot pre-mix and roll as specified" ("pre-mix" is the tar preparation for tarmac). The same company was awarded a contract to "provide, spread and compact granular material as instructed by the officer in charge" ("granular material" is murram). The area engineer in the relevant district was supposed to supervise and certify the work.

Three months after the award of the contract, but before any work was done, he wrote to his Permanent Secretary forwarding "detailed measurements of the work done by the contractors." His superior officer certified this letters as" correct for payment" to the tune of Ug. 150m/=. Attached to all these documents was a summary sheet of the work done. The cheques were duly prepared in favour of the company. What is interesting is that the processing period, that is the time from the letter of the area engineer in an up-country district to the preparation of the cheques, took four working days, which is very rare in this kind of transaction. Unfortunately, for the payees and their accomplices, the payments were intercepted and the cheques seized by the IGG. As a result, the Permanent Secretary, who was the accounting officer, was demoted, the company was blacklisted and never got any other government contract, and all the officers who were involved were disciplined.

Inflated transport costs for machinery imported from India

A company was improperly awarded a contract to transport equipment from India at the cost of $91,310 per piece, the total price was $108,700. Investigations revealed that the company was charging between $11,000 and $14,000 per 20 foot container from Bombay to Mombasa, when the actual rate was between $3,000 and $4,000. The IGG stopped payment to the company until they submitted invoices with the correct rates.

Settlements out of court involving fraudulent claims of $4.8 million

A project contract for construction of an industrial food technology and ceramics research centre was signed in 1978. It dragged on for more than ten years and was abandoned at foundation level.

When the client failed to pay, the construction company then put in claims for work worth over $4.8 million. The advocates of the company filed a suit in court. The law firm representing the company happened to be that of the Minister of Justice and Attorney General. The Attorney General's chambers quickly admitted liability on behalf of the government. The IGG objected and advised the Treasury not to release the money in case a settlement out of court was entered into.

The IGG also advised the Attorney General on the correct sum due to the company, and what defence to file in court. A hearing date for the case was fixed and the Attorney General's chambers put in half-hearted efforts in defence of the government case. As a matter of fact, one of the main witnesses summoned by the government side was known to have died a year before. Government lost the case and no appeal was made.

In the meantime, a reshuffle of Ministers took place and a new Minister of Justice/Attorney General was appointed. The Supreme Court allowed an appeal out of time and awarded exactly the amount we had recommended to be paid to the company. The Chief Justice, Mr. S.W.W. Wambuzi, made the following remarks in the Supreme Court:

> Before I take leave on this appeal, however, I must express my dismay at the manner in which the suit was conducted in the lower court. I get the impression that the chambers of the appellant put in a half-hearted defence so as to press the expected result with the stamp of a decision of the court. I am particularly surprised that the arguments put before us by counsel for the appellant were not advanced in the court below. On the facts of this case as they appear on the record, some of the issues raised before us arise naturally and require no particular legal prowess to discover. I have no objection to parties settling their disputes outside the law courts. In fact, parties should be encouraged to do so, but I take exception to the courts being used to stamp deals already worked out by the parties as decisions of the court.

The success in this case was facilitated by the fact that before the appeal to the Supreme Court could be made, the Minister of Justice/Attorney

General had been dropped from Cabinet, the Solicitor General had been retired, and the State Attorney handling this case had been dismissed.

Mismanagement at a cooperative transport union

Investigations were conducted into the affairs of a union which was experiencing many unexplained problems. The investigations revealed that management had no control over the operations of the union mainly because senior officers were themselves involved in corrupt practices. Each officer did what benefited him personally rather than what benefited the union. It was discovered that through manipulation of accounts, the facts were hidden from union members and the public. For example, a substantial profit for 1989/90 was declared, when in fact a large loss had been incurred. The auditors had also been corrupted by being paid a large sum of money not reflected in the accounts. The general manager had himself appropriated a union lorry and used union funds for its repair and maintenance.

Union officials borrowed a substantial amount of money through credit notes which were later destroyed. Bad debts, outright embezzlement and fraud were rampant. As a result of the IGG's investigation, disciplinary measures were taken against many officials, and police investigations followed with a view to having some officials prosecuted.

Equipment imported for Government appropriated by private companies

Investigations revealed that some private companies were using government machinery and equipment to undertake construction projects without paying for their use. Some of these machines were taken when they were brand new. But they were nowhere registered as government-owned. Few of them were recovered, and measures were to make the private users pay for that equipment.

"Ghost" workers in the Public Service

One Ministry was selected because its institutions, though spread throughout the whole country, are concentrated in a given area due to the nature of the services it renders to the general public. Investigations covering 66 institutions in half the country revealed that out of a total work force of 15,900 registered employees, 4,190 did not exist and only

11,710 could be accounted for. It was expected that once the over 4,000 "ghost" workers were eliminated, a large saving of public funds would be realised. The exercise eventually covered other areas of expenditure by the Ministry and the whole country, resulting in substantial public expenditure reductions in that Ministry.

Pre–shipment inspection services

Due mainly to the dissatisfaction of the business community with the monopoly of the firm executing the current contract, the government introduced competition in the pre-shipment inspection services (PIS). Tenders were invited under the chairmanship of the Uganda Revenue Authority (URA).

(a) It was established that one of the tenderers had manipulated the tendering process from within the URA and other institutions with influence on the awarding of the tender to ensure that their position in Uganda is consolidated.
(b) The evaluation team had given unreasonably high marks to one firm to make their position over the competitors unassailable.
(c) Tendering procedures were changed after the evaluation exercise was completed and recommendations made by the evaluation team. This was designed to favour certain firms but more especially the favoured firm.

As a result of these findings, the IGG recommended re-tendering of the PIS, but this time through the Central Tender Board (CTB). All those who participated in the previous evaluation were not to take part.

However, the Ministry of Finance kept quiet about the matter. No tendering was done; and no tender award was given. When a situation like this happens, it indicates collusion by the Ministry in the malpractices which take place in the tendering process.

Livestock Services Project (Ministry of Agriculture)

Investigations were carried out in response to a complaint from the American Ambassador to Uganda, Mr. Johnie Carson. Information received was that the contract had been awarded to an Australian firm even though the American firm's offer was US$ 400,000 less than the Australian firm's. On the technical side, the two firms were more or less equally ranked.

The IGG established that the tender had been awarded to a more expensive firm and that the tender evaluation was manipulated in favour of that firm. From the evaluation sheets of four officers who were involved in the evaluation exercise, it was clear that they were biased in favour of the Australian firm. For example, both the Australian firm and the American firm presented the same candidate as one of the resource persons. He was given more marks in the evaluation of the Australian firm than in the American one, yet the CV was the same.

The established government procedures had not been followed, as CTB had been sidelined. The IGG recommended that re-tendering should be done through CTB. The above four officers were barred from participation in the subsequent evaluation of this nature.

Re-tendering was done and the American firm emerged the winner. However, again because the Ministry was in collusion with the perpetrators of the malpractices, the tender was never awarded to the winning firm.

Misappropriation of veterinary drugs by Ministry of Agriculture, Animal Industry and Fisheries

This case concerns misappropriation of animal drugs, Clexon and Supona Extra, procured by the government of Uganda using a Japanese line of credit. Ushs. 90,822,887 could not be accounted for.

The matter was handed over to CID and some of the officers were arrested. The case was still in court at the time of writing of this paper.

Consulting services for budget and treasury functions

Invitation letters were sent on 17 December 1992 to consulting firms to submit proposals for consultancy services for the Uganda Government programme to strengthen the budget function and treasury department.

After evaluation of the technical proposals four firms emerged with the following points:

1. Total marks (%): 63.56; 62.06; 73.25; 68.25.

The Ministry of Finance wanted to proceed and negotiate with the firm that scored 73.25% without first opening financial proposals presented by the other firms. The IGG objected to this, arguing that cost was an important factor in the circumstances of the Ugandan situation.

Together with CTB, the IGG advocated that the price should always be considered when determining the evaluation criteria. This had not been done in this case.

The IGG contended that the World Bank guidelines are not an immutable law that must be followed even under the specific Ugandan circumstances, since they may be extremely disadvantageous to the country. And yet even the World Bank "two envelope" approach does not recommend this procedure of calling for price separately when prices are not to be compared.

The IGG further put it to the Minister of Finance that when the two proposals were requested for in separate sealed envelopes, it was obvious that the financial proposals could be considered in line with Para 2.36 and 2.37 of the World Bank guidelines (1982). The Ministry was adamant against comparison of the financial proposals.

The IGG also wondered why the "revised financial proposals" of the recommended firm sent after the deadline were accepted. No answer from the Ministry was made.

Why was CTB sidelined altogether from the beginning of the tendering process until the IGG started questioning the manner in which the tender was handled? Even after involving CTB, why were its decisions and guidelines rejected?

The IGG recommended that CTB should have been fully involved and that proper procedures should have been followed in the handling of this tender. All submissions should then have been made to CTB by that organisation to finalise the whole process. The role of the IGG was to monitor whether proper procedures and the regulations were being followed. Clearly they were not.

Instead of following the right procedures, the Ministry chose not to continue with the programme as originally conceived. The Ministry decided to recruit individual consultants including the consultant who was going to head the team of the recommended firm. This was another clear case of collusion using the World Bank as a bogey.

Road Project awarded to a firm which knowingly gave wrong information.

On 23 January 1993, the IGG wrote a report to the Minister responsible for this project, warning him about malpractices in the tendering process. The leading firm likely to win the tender claimed that it had planned, studied and designed a 250-kilometre road, when it had not. This misrepresentation was, however, most likely revealed by the next lowest tenderer. There was heavy lobbying at the Ministry handling the project and the ADB, and the whole process was manipulated and subverted. The IGG, therefore, advised the Minister to take a firm stand in order to show that the government would not accept manipulation of the tendering process through unethical behaviour.

The IGG called for re-tendering of the project for the following four reasons:

1. You (Ministry responsible for the project or Central Tender Board) should nullify the tendering process that has already taken place and call for fresh tenders from those firms that tendered and any other new ones that may be interested. I am making this recommendation because an award to any of the two leading firms will saddle you with a permanent accusation that the tender was manipulated and, therefore, tainted with corruption. This is so because there is no doubt that the leading firm made a misrepresentation about a project they know very well that they did not execute. Secondly, the revelation of this misrepresentation, even if it may not have been made by the next lowest tenderer, happens to be in their favour. As you know, your deputy used to work for this firm. The accusations being made against the next lowest firm are actually being made indirectly against your deputy. This oblique accusation may be unfair, but it is difficult to dismiss, just as it is difficult to accept, that a tender should be awarded to a company which intentionally told lies without caring about the harm this act would do to its reputation, and its prospects of doing business with the government.
2. If government does not take a firm stand against manipulation of the tendering process, either through the misrepresentation of information or through unethical lobbying of public officials, then government will send a wrong signal to the business community about its position on corruption. It is, therefore, imperative that government should take this opportunity to show that unethical practices are not acceptable and no one will be allowed to benefit from such behaviour.
3. I understand the Bank has taken a position on who should be awarded the tender, irrespective of whether our tendering process has been subverted. I think that this is a wrong position for a tender to take. The Bank should encourage strict adherence to rules and regulations, both of the Bank and government, concerning tenders. It has no right to dictate to government not to put its house in order. However, the Bank can easily exploit our own markets. The Bank should get a

clear message that its advice will be acceptable when it encourages transparency, not when it sides with those who attempt to subvert our system.

4. It would not be right to award the tender to the second lowest firm, either, in view of the likelihood of undermining the reputation of your deputy. The best option is to re-tender so that there is an opportunity to handle the tendering process as meticulously as possible and with the necessary circumspection. The firms affected should, when re-tendering, also have an opportunity to prove that they are actually the best. All firms which tendered earlier should be allowed to re-tender along with those that did not. Government might benefit from the expected improvements in all the tenders.

There was no reaction to these recommendations of the IGG. However, after one year of silence and no action taken, the IGG received a copy of a letter from the Permanent Secretary of the Ministry informing the CTB that the award to the leading firm had been upheld by government "in spite of government's earlier objections arising out of some irregularities in the proposal." Meanwhile, CTB had been ignored and the relevant Ministers awarded the tender and went ahead to communicate to ADB that the tender had been awarded in spite of earlier government objections. The fact of this award was neither communicated to CTB nor to the IGG, who were now to have pointed out the malpractices which took place.

This was the wrong signal to show the seriousness of government in handling corruption. In a meeting held by the Ministry responsible for this project, the chairman informed the meeting that the Ministry learned at a later date that the leading firm's technical proposal contained information which appeared to be false. The apparent falsehood was to do with a project purported to have been done by the consultant, but which independent investigation showed had never been done. He went on to say that "should that have been discovered during the technical evaluation stage, the proposal would have been rejected and declared non-responsive outright," that is, the firm would have been disqualified. When the consultant appeared before the same meeting, he informed the members that after his attention was drawn to the false project aspect, "he cross-checked his documentation and noted that this road appeared erroneously in a long list of 27 projects with a heading 'Completed Project'," that is, he admitted that his firm had told a lie. There is, therefore, no doubt that government was aware of the misrepresentation by the leading firm.

The importance of the 250-kilometre false road project is that it is the only major road claimed, though falsely, that is comparable to the project being tendered for. The others are short roads in housing estates and are not relevant for a project of the size of the project in this tender which is 319 kilometres long.

Worse still, we were informed that "Because of the time lag, slight variations in the original contract price may be expected," that is, the price will now rise. But why was there this long time lag? Who is responsible for it? The IGG wrote to the Minister and for a year no action was taken, but eventually the action taken was to confirm the tendering malpractices.

The recommendations of the IGG were ignored and the leading firm was still awarded the tender. The part played by ADB was unfortunate and the IGG made the following comment: "How can ADB, in which we are members, force us to accept malpractices which violate government rules, regulations and procedures?" The award "sends the wrong signal to the business community that government is lax on tendering malpractices, even those it is aware of." Up to now, no remedial measures have been taken and none will be taken, since the contract is being executed by the firm known to have been involved in malpractices.

Conclusion

If the political leadership tolerates or even encourages corruption, for example, if the political leadership is not ready to punish those who are corrupt within its own group, then corruption will be encouraged and it will become uncontrollable. Corruption cannot exist without the connivance, even if passive, of the political leadership. It diverts official decision-making from what a decision should have been to what it should not have been. Corruption leads to discriminatory dispensation of government services, and to the distortion of the economy through the misallocation and wastage of resources. It introduces discrimination and arbitrariness in decision-making so that rules, regulations and procedures become unimportant. In extreme cases, decision-making is not only transferred to the corruptors, but it is hijacked by, or arrogated to them. Where countries are concerned, sovereignty is completely surrendered.

Corruption can only be eliminated when both the political leadership and the public make a concerted effort not to tolerate it any more. But where the State is soft on corruption, people may be reluctant to uphold laws which get in the way of their personal or sectional interests. The burden, therefore, must fall on the political actors who are the only individuals with the power to bring about a stronger allegiance to the State and, hence, a commitment to the national interest.

7 The Responsibilities of the Government, the Media, and the Public in Combating Corruption

Damian Kato

The responsibilities of government, the media and the public in combating corruption are important topics that need to be discussed together if only to identify the ways in which the respective parties can help and complement each other to contain corruption. Corruption has bedevilled governments and countries not only in Africa but the world over and its effects are devastating. Corruption shoots up costs and diverts resources from their productive use. For example, if citizens have been expecting a hospital, a road, or a school in some place, they will not get any of those projects when there is corruption because the resources which have been allocated for these purposes are eaten up or diverted by the corrupt officials. Also, because of the increase in costs, additional funds cannot subsequently be mobilised to complete the projects.

The sum total is that citizens cannot educate their children or have health services. Neither can they engage in serious productive activity due to the lack of proper communication, and so on. The ramifications are great. Corruption is therefore a threat to the political, economic and social development of our countries. To confront the problem, a concerted effort must be made by the government, the media and the public, as well as many other concerned parties.

Responsibilities of government

Good Governance

One of the cardinal responsibilities of the government is to govern competently. In doing so, the government must inevitably be transparent and accountable for its actions. This is especially true, given the fact that the government is maintained by the public who pay taxes to run it. Once the government is transparent and accountable, there is every likelihood that it will be efficient and responsive to public opinion. In Uganda, one of the areas that is likely to enhance transparency and accountability, and thus competent government, is the enforcement of the leadership code of conduct.

Related to competence, transparency, and accountability is the need to empower institutions such as the Inspector General of Government (IGG) and to ensure that those things which may not be going well are rectified in the interests of good governance to oversee the management of government affairs. Also related to competence is the need for the government to create a good political enabling climate for the operations of private anti-corruption institutions. In Uganda, under the current administration, private anti--corruption crusaders proliferate due to such a political climate. The press, for instance, has now started plunging into investigative journalism which augurs well for the anti-corruption crusade.

Professional Civil Service

The second responsibility of the government is to ensure that it develops a professional civil service. This can only be done by blocking loopholes for corruption and encouraging self-esteem and commitment to work among all categories of public servants. To do this the government needs to enhance remuneration of public servants to living wage levels so that they have no excuse for engaging in corrupt practices.

Payment of a living wage is a crucial factor in making public employees efficient and in restraining them from indulging in malpractices. Public servants should also be trained from time to time so that they have skills to do their work competently and honestly. Related to this, the government must ensure that public servants have a code of conduct prescribing the minimum standard of conduct expected of them. Public and private activities should not be mixed up. The purpose of a code of conduct is to avoid distortions that can affect the clarity and efficiency of an individual's actions, thereby avoiding potential acts of corruption.

Professional Security Service

The third responsibility of government is to ensure the development of a professional security service comprising the army, police and prison services as well as other security agencies. This is necessary if corruption is to be fought. Security personnel can be prone to corruption if they are not properly looked after and if they do not have a proper code of conduct. The promotion of their welfare as well as codes of conduct are necessary ingredients for their upright behaviour. Coupled with this is, of course, training. This too is a major factor in moulding their behaviour and attitudes towards corruption.

Sound Economy

The government is responsible for establishing proper political, fiscal and monetary policies to create a sound economy. The government must ensure that the economy is not run-down, otherwise what will ensue is widespread poverty. Poverty forces people not only to tolerate corruption, but also to initiate it. Also, the more the government intervenes in the economy, the more opportunities are provided for corruption to flourish. This is because government intervention is usually accompanied by so many regulations, some of them very difficult to administer and often making the processing of transactions cumbersome. Besides, many of the responsibilities assumed by government clearly lie beyond its capabilities. Therefore, the privatisation or divestiture programme leading to steady government disengagement from playing a prominent role in the economy is, in my view, a welcome measure in the struggle against corruption.

Delivery of Services

The government also has a responsibility to ensure delivery of services to its people if corruption is to be curbed. In particular, infrastructural services such as roads cannot be easily organised by individual citizens. These infrastructural services are necessary to enable the people to engage in productive economic activities for their welfare and development and for the development of the economy as well, thereby alleviating poverty which can foster corruption.

Education

If corruption is to be fought, the education of the public is a crucial factor in this endeavour. It is therefore the government's responsibility to see that this is done. The strategy should be pursued on two levels; namely education of children in school and education of the public in general. In Uganda the government is pursuing both. For instance, in 1987 the government set up an education policy review commission to inquire into the policies governing education in Uganda with a view to improving them. The government, in its White Paper, based on the commission report, endorsed the policy recommendation regarding "Promotion in schools of such values as honesty, sense of responsibility, integrity in the use of public funds and property, love for productive and constructive work, and respect for those who labour to produce material, intellectual, and social wealth."[1] This was in recognition of the fact that if we are going to produce and sustain a good society, the children, who are the future leaders, should be imbued with moral, ethical, and spiritual values and they must be taught to develop self-discipline, integrity, tolerance and human fellowship.

Responsibility of the Media

The responsibility of the media in combating corruption cannot be over-emphasized. The advantage the media is that they have a wide audience at short notice. They can reach the population easily through circulation of their newspapers or through radio and television.

Educational Responsibility

One of the responsibilities of the media is in the educational field. The media could, for instance, allocate space in their papers for advertisements geared at educating the public about the dangers of corruption. Cannot the media arrange this? In the newspapers there is a children's corner. Cannot newspaper editors publish stories for children that can teach them to be crusaders in anti-corruption activities?

Investigative Responsibility

The media also has an investigative responsibility in our struggle to fight corruption. This responsibility is in the area of investigative journalism. However, there is a need for this to be handled responsibly. The existence of a responsible press is an essential factor not only for the fight against corruption but for sustaining democracy and the respect of human rights. The press can play a key role in the battle to keep government and the public service honest. To be able to play this role well, the media needs to improve its skills. The media must also encourage self-discipline within itself through development of an appropriate code of ethics. Besides, it is the responsibility of journalists to see that they are not corrupted themselves, otherwise they will have no moral authority to condemn those who are corrupt.

Rewards

Many media institutions make money through the sale of newspapers and advertisement, and so on. It is their responsibility to part with some of this money and promote good governance by giving rewards to people who come out with concrete evidence against those who are corrupt. Rewards can entice the population to join the anti-corruption campaign.

Collaboration with Anti-Corruption Agencies:

Finally, in fighting corruption, the media has the responsibility to collaborate with other anti-corruption agencies, particularly those which can enforce sanctions, such as the IGG. Quite often we follow articles of allegations of corruption published in newspapers. However, when we try to investigate the allegations we do not get very far because the papers do not give enough information and evidence. It is necessary for the media to join hands with the anti–corruption agencies to further the anti-corruption campaign.

Responsibilities of the public

The government and media institutions are not solely responsible for the fight against corruption. Individuals and civil society, including other non-governmental and non-profit organisations, must have the opportunity to present their complaints and inquiries regarding, not only government agencies and public servants, but also the private sector and its employees. How can the public access information regarding corruption to the IGG? This can be done in a number of ways.

First, the public can make a formal report to the IGG by writing to the office. Second, one can call at the IGG's office and make a report verbally although this will need to be followed by a written statement. Third, one can go through the press. Articles published on corruption in the press are followed up by the office for investigation. In addition, sometimes the Inspector General of Government appears on live-talk radio where questions and complaints are answered.

Finally, in the fight against corruption, the public and government have a joint responsibility of civic education. The government alone cannot promote awareness at all levels incorporating concepts of ethics, honesty, and responsibility. The public, and particularly parents, are crucial. They have to bring up their children well. Such an educational effort by the public and government will create future generations capable of resisting corruption.

8 The Role of the Inspector General of Government

Matthias B. Tumwesigye

Background to the Function of the Office of the Inspector General of Government (IGG)

During the colonial period there was no responsibility for, or serious involvement in, incidents of corruption by the indigenous people employed in the public service as all major decisions were made by colonial officials. There were no representative institutions during the colonial period and, therefore, public control, accountability, or criticism of public officials was unknown. After independence, the new rulers took over a colonial state which was controlled by excessive use of force and they perpetuated the colonial state rather than making it responsive to the people. To make matters worse, soon after independence, the democratic process was overthrown by misuse of the army and police.

Corruption, therefore, soon emerged not merely out of economic greed but also from the necessity of political survival since the basis of continued support for the politicians was generally patronage sustained by the continuous flow of favours to one's followers. The awarding of contracts which, before independence, was monopolised by colonial officials, was the first eye opener to the favours that can be bestowed by the holders of public office. These contracts involved the construction of roads, schools, public buildings, radio and TV stations, hotels and others. The public sector was also expanded by formation of numerous parastatals, which were further quantitatively increased by the expropriation of Asian properties after the expulsion of Asians in 1972.

Prior to 1986 this country was faced with a history in which human rights, including the right to life and the right to property, were virtually non-existent. Systems of control, accountability and management broke down during these periods of dictatorship and chaotic rule. Instability and insecurity of job tenure set in as a result of the political upheavals of the time. Corruption was also exacerbated by an expanding population in conditions of a contracting economy and worsening standards of living.

Corruption had been elevated to the level of an ideology, the culture of success in politics, in religion, in business, and public administration. People in all facets of life embraced this ideology with enthusiasm at the expense of integrity which should be the hallmark of distinction. Honesty and integrity had become a "vice" to be scoffed at; dishonesty and cunning were "virtues" to be cultivated and emulated.

A successful thief or swindler of yesterday became the successful politician and leader of today. Everything was upside down. Corruption had become systematic, it was a recognised way of life, and a respectable one at that.

Hence within a short time after independence corruption permeated every sphere of public life and the population became resigned to it as an inevitable way of life. "Man eats where he works" became the common household phrase. Worse still, corruption extended even to "eating where one did not work". This came to be known as "air supply," or getting paid for goods not supplied or services not rendered.

So, by 1986, corruption was generally considered one of the primary problems facing the country though, officially, it was not acknowledged to exist.

Public service is a public trust and, over the years, this trust had been abused by public officials. Indeed at the time the office of the IGG was formed the population had been yearning for a clean government for a long time. Point No. 7 of the 10-Point Programme of NRM government is about the elimination of corruption and the misuse of power. In full it says the following:

> Africa, being a continent that is never in shortage of problems, has also the problem of corruption, particularly bribery and misuse of office to serve personal interests. Corruption is indeed a problem that ranks with the problems of structural distortions that we have been talking about.

We have just referred to the way in which corruption can revitalise any disease, for example, when medical staff divert government drugs for private sale. Consequently the patients do not get adequate treatment, thus leading to slow recovery or other health complications or, in extreme cases, even death.

In development planning or trade, a cheaper option can be ignored in preference to a costly one because the officials concerned stand to gain. Corruption induced decisions can therefore cause distortions of great magnitude.

Therefore, to enable the tackling of our backwardness, corruption must be eliminated once and for all. This is what defined the main mission of the institution of the IGG as the problem of corruption had assumed gigantic proportions. It had become the main channel of contacts between public officials and those they are supposed to serve. Corruption had totally undermined the rights of the people. Everything had become a privilege to be paid for; there were no rights. This mainly affected the poor and the financially weak who are the majority of the people.

This is the difficult situation the office of the IGG found itself faced with at the beginning of its work against corruption. Compared to the armed struggle the NRM waged to capture power, this was a more difficult struggle. In armed conflict the enemy is easily identifiable, the weapons are relatively easy to procure and the rules are easy to work out or to adapt. The solution is also clear; it can be total defeat of the enemy, peace talks or some form of arbitration by third parties. On the other hand, in the struggle against corruption, you are completely encircled, highly infiltrated, the enemy is not clearly defined and the weapons are not so clear or easily available. Our success has therefore depended on the concerted efforts made by both the political leadership and the press and the public not to tolerate corruption any more.

As already stated above one of the primary objectives of the current administration since its inception was the elimination of corruption and abuse of power. This is important because corruption cannot exist without the connivance of the political leadership, even if passive. If the political leadership tolerates or condones corruption, for example, if there is no strong will to punish those who are corrupt within its own group, then corruption will flourish and it will become uncontrollable. The backing and the political will of the leadership are a prerequisite for any anti-corruption strategy to succeed.

At the beginning of the current administration the greatest departure from the past was that the political leadership at the highest levels was strongly against corruption and gave all support to anti-corruption measures. This is what led to the formation of the IGG's office and the resuscitation of existing institutions which had become dormant for a long time. In order to reduce the tolerance of corruption, it was clearly sensible to mobilise the public against corruption. Unfortunately the initial momentum against corruption has somewhat slowed down and this is one of the major problems to deal with.

The determination of the political leadership to fight corruption earned it the co-operation and support of the public without which no anti-corruption efforts can succeed. When the public woke up and understood the dangers posed by corruption, they began to dictate the pace of the anti-corruption activities. In 1989, for example, 121 civil servants were dismissed as a result of the outcry of the press and the public which forced the PAC of Parliament and Cabinet to act decisively. About half of these were customs officials. Numerous senior officials have been dismissed or prosecuted in response to public pressure. Political leaders also have been relieved of their appointments as a result of public pressure. However, the public remains dissatisfied and keeps on pressing for harsher punishments to be meted out to those deemed to be corrupt. But the country's legal machinery is still greatly lopsided in favour of the corrupt.

Whereas in the developed countries corruption is dealt with in a swift and severe manner and the relevant institutions can be depended upon to invoke the law in the national interest, in Uganda this is not yet the case. In fact, for sometime now there has developed a gap between verbal and policy condemnation of corruption and the adoption of effective measures to thwart it. Policy measures which promote social reform and curb corruption have been half-hearted because some of the leaders have a vested interest in perpetuating corruption. This is why there is disillusionment, resentment and scepticism about the ongoing efforts to fight corruption. Some of the leaders have lost credibility, and this is what is making it urgent to take stronger measures to restore public support.

9 Good Governance and Control of Corruption

James Kahoza

Corruption is a social vice that is as old as society itself. It is therefore reasonable to say that it is not possible to get rid of it. It is true that its incidence gets less and less as man advances in terms of control on the use of power and civilised conduct.

In simple terms, corruption is the use of a public asset for personal (private) gain. The word "asset" has a slightly different meaning from that implied in the accounting profession. In this context, "asset" means power, office or influence. Personal gain may mean financial or material gain or simply personal gratification.

What is corrupt conduct seems to be identifiable in all cultures and religions in modern terms. Fortunately, it does seem that all religions and cultures show a fairly high level of ethical consensus on management of social affairs. This ethical consensus observed the world over has something to do with the inherent character of man but is also a result of a global culture fostered by a revolution in mass communications.

Why is corruption such a public concern? This is perhaps because democratic/representative governance is now the rule rather than the exception in the modern world. There is a growing perception that governments should substantially reflect not just what is in the public interest, but what is also good or ethical. This does not just relate to government but also to the individuals who hold offices in it.

Corruption takes a variety of forms. It expresses itself in the form of gifts, bribes, extortion, abuse of office, nepotism, or even certain forms of theft.

Gifts: Gifts take many forms. There is what could be called pressure-free gifts. Here, the gift is given by a personal friend or a business associate out of friendship, and there is no intention or understanding implicit or explicit that the gift is given to trigger or influence official action. There are, however, gifts which are not pressure-free. These are given by those who work with or provide services to official or private entities and are aimed at buying favours or access to services. Whatever form they take, gifts should be discouraged because, under certain conditions, the recipient may be forced to make decisions that are less than impartial. Indeed, some countries have laws which restrict public officials as to what gifts they can accept and those they cannot.

It is difficult to ascertain that a gift even when given by a friend has not determined or will not determine a decision or policy, nor will observers resist the perception that the gift is given with the goal of influencing the receiver. It does not follow that a gift will be exchanged for a favour. What is however damaging is the nature of public perception especially when a government is involved. There are few government actions or decisions that the public does not view with suspicion. It can however be said without much contradiction that most gifts are given to buy favours, which is a corrupt intent.

Bribes: Bribes are more explicit than gifts. A bribe is given to influence an action. It is given on the basis of an understanding. It is therefore patently criminal in nature. Bribes distort proper functioning of the market; they misallocate resources; they violate principles of justice and fair play; they disregard merit, and reward premeditated wrong doing. In many countries, bribes dominate the infrastructure of corruption.

Abuse of office or privilege: Any office, public or private, confers power on the holder. It is probably true to say that all forms of corruption are facilitated by power, political, financial, or bureaucratic, but power also confers discretion on those who wield it. Power is abused when it is used to attain what is illegal or unethical, but even where discretion is allowed in law, it can be and is usually used in a manner that is unethical. Discretionary actions or decisions are not usually illegal but they are perceived to be unethical and can bring sanctions on an official especially in a democratic society. In Uganda and most African countries, abuse of power is very common and is fostered by the low level of awareness in society as a whole. Abuse of office is a term that has no equivalent expression in African languages and is therefore not understood by the uneducated. The problem here is not language but the level of education among virtually the entire population.

Conflict of interest: Conflict of interest exists in any society. It can take a financial, ethnic or regional character. Religions prohibit serving two masters and in the ancient world, Greek and Roman rulers usually discouraged holding of offices that could create conflict at an individual level. These days, we see conflict of interest in government and also in private business. In Uganda, individuals hold official positions while at the same time doing business. It is common to find officials channelling public contracts to businesses owned by them even though there is a law against such practice. In the private sector, officials engage in inside trading for the benefit of side businesses which they personally own with their families to the disadvantage of the organisations they represent.

What has been said so far is familiar to those who enforce public accountability. For some of us who come from developing countries, the problem is not just about dealing with corruption, but rather getting the subject understood at all. It is probably correct to state that accountability or lack of it are middle-class terms. It is the middle class which created the need to account largely because of the nature of their economic activities. It is the middle class in Europe which put together public resources and also formed public companies to invest in manufacturing and commerce and created interests stretching from England to the Hapsburg Empire in central Europe.

The emergence and development of finance capital demanded the creation of an accounting profession. This profession was introduced in educational institutions in order to train manpower to examine the conduct of managers of companies and advise shareholders if their capital was well managed and safe and earning more money. Side by side with the accounting profession, there developed other professions like law, medicine and many others. The professions had therefore to develop professional ethics since they were not just serving themselves, but also the public. They put out documents containing ethical codes for each profession enshrining the duties and responsibilities of that particular profession. Professional ethics, therefore, came to be defined as the sum total of laws governing a profession and the values and norms on which those codes are based as well as ethical principles which guide professional conduct.

In my society, for instance, what is ethical is not always clear to the majority of the population. They understand what is immoral or unjust, but not necessarily what is unethical, because when one talks of ethics, one then talks in professional language. The majority of the population consists of illiterate peasants among whom the word "corruption" makes no sense in the context of traditional culture. So, how does one deal with corruption within the context of the African social environment?

Even though the very large majority of the people in Africa lack the language of professionals and do not get the content of what we understand as corruption, those people who practise it in government and in business do understand it fully. There is no doubt that they take advantage of people's ignorance to avoid accountability. This is the very essence of the problem. It is public opinion which forces a government to keep in line and to account to the population. Public opinion on crucial matters of corruption is very weak in an undeveloped society. Newspapers inform a very small segment of society and even those who could read papers are cut off due to lack of communication.

There is no evidence that there is any strong correlation between corruption and poverty while it would be correct to observe a relation between corruption and the level of education and culture in any society.

Good Governance: What do we mean when we talk of good governance? We live in a society that has over time evolved from a stone-age condition to the present technological society and at every stage in that evolutionary process, there have been governments of some description. It is reasonable to say that at every stage in history, people ranked governments differently depending on the social beliefs and customs of the governed. We should also consider what confers on the ruler the right to govern. Way back in history, power - physical power - call it military force, gave a ruler the right to rule, but even then, military rulers, who in most cases also became kings with hereditary rights, were judged in relation to each other with regard to quality of their rule.

No less important is the question of how the ruler related to the ruled. Did he represent and defend their security and interests? Security of the people was the most important even though the rights of people as individuals were not always well defined. The extent to which these rights were observed or violated depended very much on the character of the ruler. Since there was no constitution or clear system of law, each ruler determined the fate of the individual and also whether divergent views could or could not be tolerated.

The ideas of democracy came to be felt in Europe when the middle classes demanded representative governments during the 18th and 19th centuries. It would perhaps be right to say that good governance implies representative government. These days, however, there are more issues about good governance than representative government. Indeed, representation now means a lot more than it meant during the 18th century in Europe. We now take the view that the right to represent people must be derived from popular mandates freely given by the people through free and fair elections. So, free elections also have a lot to do with good governance. There are other things that go with good governance. There is a free press, free speech, the right to associate and other rights which these days are considered fundamental and inviolable. These topics have been discussed at various international fora in the framework of the United Nations for decades, and even though these rights are accepted by all, they are not, in practice, allowed by all governments.

There is little doubt now that what good governance means is universally agreed. It can perhaps rightly be said that the collapse of communist regimes in Europe showed that a society where different political opinions are not allowed free expression is fundamentally flawed and therefore unstable. In countries, attempts have been made in the past to emulate the political virtues of one party democracy, and in some developing countries such attempts are still being made. What is generally not recognised is that there cannot be democracy without the right to choose, that is to say, the right to examine different political views and choose the one each person wants through the secret ballot.

We should not think that political parties are in themselves a guarantee for democracy. A couple of powerful political parties in a country can, with the use of large financial resources, turn themselves into corrupt oligarchies with total monopoly of power. It is probably not inaccurate to say that in some countries such a situation currently exists.

It is pointless to pretend that good governance as understood today can exist without a freely elected parliament, because an elected parliament lies at the heart of any system of integrity that can express popular interest and enforce accountability on those who rule. A free and fair election is important here because a parliament which consists of people who have rigged, bribed, or bought their way into the House has no legitimacy and is itself a part of corruption.

Disclosure of corrupt practices on the part of the executive by any citizen can lead to court litigation on account of slander. Even in advanced societies, people or newspapers usually refrain from direct accusation of corruption against any government official. This is where Parliament is important. It is free from prosecution, so are statements of members in the House. Parliaments therefore can hold executives accountable on a day-to-day basis. But Parliament is not important in itself. What is even more important is its composition with regard to opposing political views.

Control of Corruption: Corruption is a social vice that will not go away any time soon. Even in countries that are considered relatively clean, it still occurs. It is therefore necessary to find legal and institutional mechanisms to contain it. To begin with, it is important to get the people to know what it is that makes us look at corruption as socially unacceptable. The task of making people aware should go beyond the confines of religion because morality and ethics are very closely related but not synonymous.

My experience in Uganda, and by extension the whole of Africa, is that people, even those who are well educated, do not know much about ethical demands imposed on them by their offices. It is true that those who have had training in formal professions like medicine, law or accountancy know what their ethics demand, but beyond these, others do not take ethics as important or, to put it more correctly, are not familiar with ethical matters that relate to their jobs or businesses.

I believe that we should start with students while still at school and continue with ethics as a subject to be taught like others. It should be taught to all students because our present educational systems do not emphasise or even teach it at all, so much so that a graduate in history, physics, or geology may know absolutely nothing about ethics and yet he or she may at one time or other hold offices that demand exercise of ethical judgement.

In a country like USA, ethics has an important place in government even though I have yet to learn if it is taught in American schools as a subject. The American government, however, has established ethics for officers at all levels so that most official decisions are subjected to ethical tests before they come out. There is no doubt that the existence of these offices has had a significant impact on the reduction of corruption in United States administration.

Ethics, as pointed out, is different from morality. What is relevant here is the type of ethics which make demands on public officials while providing a public service. This is why our concern should relate to public institutions - governments or public companies. What then should ethics teach to those holding public offices? The teaching should start with the principle of respectability with regard to how one values oneself. The act of placing a value on oneself will also make a holder of a public office realise that one has to guard public confidence in and integrity of the office so as to reflect what one considers to be honourable.

Education in ethics should also guard against using one's office in a manner that creates the appearance of impropriety or act in such a way as to undermine public confidence and integrity of government. Equally important is the principle of accountability. This involves the way decisions are made, how resources are managed, or how power is acquired and used. Decisions that are not made on merit are partial and probably made for gain and resources not properly accounted for were probably not employed in the interest of public service. Education in ethics should also put emphasis on democracy and the value of popular leadership as well as the need for those in power to observe the law without fear or favour.

Ethics education is important in the fight to control corruption. When awareness about ethics and corruption is imparted to young people at the school level, there is a better chance of producing people who grow up respecting their offices. Such people will probably not look at official ethical demands on them as mere inconveniences. For a long time now, governments have employed substantial resources and legal mechanisms to fight corruption. While this is no doubt correct, few countries have paid much attention to the teaching of ethics as a part of education to their citizens.

The most common weapon against corruption is anti-corruption legislation which is no doubt the most effective. Such legislation usually has ethical objectives but also empowers those who are supposed to enforce the law. Ethical objectives of any legislation usually defines what an upright official should look like.

It is important for any legislation to pay attention to public confidence, fairness, integrity in decision making, and lastly efficiency in government service. The law should prohibit actions by officials who by their conduct reduce confidence in government and therefore affect voluntary compliance with government policy instructions. Equally, failure to treat people's needs equally implies personal interest on the part of the public official. Any law should be very clear as to what conduct is unacceptable in a public officer. Anti-corruption laws usually prohibit bribery, extortion, graft, conflict of interest and so on, but even in this case, a law will not, cannot, give a watertight definition of what constitutes wrong-doing especially as cultures differ from country to country.

The legislation should also empower enforcement institutions by giving power to those charged with the responsibility of fighting corruption. In some countries, specific laws against corruption do not exist. Since corruption goes beyond the confines of the Penal Code contained in the laws of all countries, fighting it calls for separate laws which target all facets of corruption. In many countries, the constitution creates an office to deal with corruption. In Uganda, a department of Inspectorate of Government, or Ombudsman as it is called in some other countries, has been created. The constitution gives the Inspector General of Government the following powers:

"(1) The Inspectorate of Government shall have power to investigate, cause investigation, cause arrest, prosecute or cause prosecution in respect of cases involving corruption, abuse of authority or of public office.
(2) The Inspector General of Government may, during the course of his or her duties or as a consequence of his or her findings, make such orders and give such directions as are necessary and appropriate in the circumstances.
(3) Subject to the provisions of any law, the Inspectorate of Government shall have power to enter and inspect the premises or property of any department of Government, person or of any authority, to call for, examine and, where necessary, retain any document or item in connection with the case being investigated, found on the premises; and may, in those premises, carry out any investigation for the purpose of its functions.
(4) The Inspectorate of Government shall, when enforcing the Leadership Code of Conduct, have all the powers conferred on it by this Chapter in addition to any other powers conferred by law.
(5) Subject to this Constitution, Parliament shall enact any law necessary for enabling the Inspectorate of Government to discharge its functions effectively and efficiently and in particular, to ensure that the discharge of those functions is not frustrated by any person or authority."

The existence of a constitutional office to fight corruption is not a guarantee of success. In Africa, the fight against corruption is particularly difficult because the civil society is still very weak. But corruption is not just doing wrong or evil. It can manifest itself in very human terms, and because it creates friendship and social obligations, it tends to be self-perpetuating. Exposing it is not easy. The demands of public interest may be counter-balanced by moral duty or personal obligations to a colleague or even self-interest where exposure can lead to retribution. At the political level, loyalty to what is considered a higher aim or unwillingness to rock the boat may indeed dictate silence.

I will discuss the problems the civil society faces in Africa. The problem facing those who fight corruption in Africa is a dual culture. You have a mass culture which is traditional and another one which is corporate, but which, even though narrow in terms of the numbers that belong to it, is more influential since it possesses intellectual and technological power. It is necessary to discuss how the two cultures in the African society as it is at the moment perceive power. I introduce power at this point because corruption as defined above is a practice which violates our sense of ethics. Every society has some form of perception of what is good and honourable.

When we talk of ethics, we talk of core values which should guide public service. Proper conduct in delivering public service should therefore satisfy ethical or moral abstractions of all men. Men therefore respect honesty, equality, integrity, impartiality, fairness, equity and such other concepts which we use to measure ethical performance. Because corruption is a violation of an ethical, and in most cases, legal demand, it needs power to facilitate it and perpetrate it.

How does traditional culture perceive power then? To the people who are uneducated, power is perceived in its raw forms. Even though leaders are now elected, the uneducated people do not consider the power they possess as accountable power. The leader therefore personifies the chief with whom the society is familiar. This state of affairs leads to two potentially dangerous developments:-

(a) The African leader knows from the time he is elected that he has very little or no burden of accountability as far as the majority of the electorate are concerned.

(b) The people who oppose his policies, and who usually belong to the professional classes will probably be looked upon by the traditional society as trouble makers. In order to get understood, they in turn appeal to tribal or ethnic sentiments.

The majority of the people in Africa do not understand the language used in the corporate culture in which corruption finds full expression. The corporate culture or the professional classes do use expressions that have little or no meaning in traditional society. We often hear of Public Trust, conflict of interest, abuse of office, or undue influence. These concepts came to gain prominence with the rise of modern capitalism, and especially the birth of public companies. During the industrial revolution in Europe and the colonisation that followed it, commercial and industrial corporations needed to exploit world resources most of which became available with colonisation. The public companies created financial markets that created a pool of financial resources owned by thousands of companies and individuals. Public companies soon dominated the whole of western Europe. This development necessitated the growth of a management class and the professions.

Each profession has a code of ethics which governs its practice. The reason for this is that those serving in the professions hold positions of trust. Either they control resources entrusted to them by the public or they have confidential information on individual members of the public which they acquire during the course of their service and which the individuals readily provide to them in confidence.

When a person is holding a position or office of trust, that person is expected to meet those demands which the public considers to be ethical. If in government, one is expected to respect the principle of public interest, the principle of objective judgement, the principle of democratic leadership, and the principle of respectability as is generally understood.

The division between state and government in African traditional forms of governance is nebulous at best and, at worst, non existent. It could not be otherwise because the differentiation between the two requires abstract thinking which is the preserve of the educated who, because of their education and training, belong, at least partly, to a different cultural environment as already pointed out.

It is not easy to deal with corruption because it is part of all social relationships which form the fabric of society. Anyone who tries to reform corruption will find himself/herself at a loss as to where to begin. Laws to fight corruption have been enacted and enforcement offices created, but these have, to say the least, had limited success. Even with organs of state which are mandated to enforce laws against corruption, a number of problems hamper their success.

- Even where a new president or head of government is determined to fight the vice of corruption, that person finds that he/she inherits a corrupt establishment, which impedes efforts to change.
- There may not be any commitment to fight corruption at the top of a government, so much so that even if the middle ranking people try to change, they are restricted by lack of commitment of the top leadership.
- Public officials tend to rely too much on enforcement laws which do not really change the way people behave and think. They rely on strict enforcement that may lead to repression and abuse of power, thus creating an environment for political revolt that frequently brings into being an even more corrupt administration.
- Most efforts to reform corrupt governments focus on smaller fry, leaving those at the top untouched and yet these are usually the most corrupt. This leads to general public disregard for the law, which then is seen as unfair and contrary to known principles of justice.
- Anti-corruption reforms face all sorts of vested interests from those who live by bending the rules in order to supplement their incomes

or simply amass wealth. Indeed, some of these people may be so powerful as to cause violence or even the overthrow of a legally established order.

There are various organs of state which take part in the process of stopping wrong-doing, corruption being one of these wrongs. Some countries have inspectors (Ombudsmen) and some rely on the other established judicial process. The idea of this office originated in ancient China and has been adopted by Scandinavian countries mainly. In terms of effectiveness in the fight against corruption, the Ombudsman can achieve a lot. In the first place, this office is more open and more easily accessible than public administrators, or courts of law. When people have grievances or their rights are violated by those in the bureaucracy, they normally resort to court litigation, but courts are slow, in fact very slow by their very nature. Courts are formal and professionally mechanistic.

The Ombudsman is more open and handy when people's complaints fall on deaf ears. According to the Transparency International Source Book, the Office of the Ombudsman "independently receives and investigates allegations of maladministration as well as examines:

(i) a decision, process, recommendation, act of omission or commission which is contrary to law, rules or regulations or is a departure from procedures, unless it is bona fide and has valid reasons; is perverse, arbitrary or unreasonable, unjust, biased, oppressive or discriminatory based on irrelevant grounds; or involves the exercise or the failure or refusal to do so for reasons of corrupt or improper motives such as bribery, jobbery, favouritism, nepotism, and administrative excesses.
(ii) Neglect, inattention, delay, incompetence, inefficiency, and ineptitude in administration or discharge of duties and responsibilities".

Such offices are very adaptable in all countries at different stages of development. The office does not only investigate corruption but also inspects systems of administration with a view to minimising corruption.

The office of the Auditor-General is, however, a very different institution. Its effectiveness in dealing with corruption is hampered by their rigid professionalism. An auditor is not and is not supposed to be a fighter. He or she observes and puts his or her statement in a very detached manner. This may be good or bad depending on your view point. It has been argued that auditors should refrain from direct accusations because otherwise they would eventually be drawn into the partisan interests and thus lose their objectivity.

It is true that the Auditors-General report their findings to parliaments in nearly all countries and expect action to be taken to correct any wrongs that may be sighted. Whether Parliament will act or not depends on the political environment in any country. Where the government has a lot of influence in parliament, accountability is usually compromised for very obvious reasons. Where nearly all members of parliament support the government, every member is a potential beneficiary of executive patronage and is unlikely to press for accountability. For these reasons, in those countries where democracy exists, the Auditor-General's reports are discussed by committees headed by members of the opposition in parliament. This is not just a British custom. There are very good reasons for it.

Auditors-General therefore have little power to fight corruption. In all countries that I know of, they have no executive power. They report to parliament and wait for the legislature to act.

This does not mean that Auditors-General do not help in fighting corruption. In fact, they help a lot in an indirect way. Their reports are public documents and, in these reports, they do expose a lot of wrong-doing that the public may not know. In so doing, they act as a deterrent to corruption. Legally, this may be all they can do in the fight against corruption.

Part Four

LOCAL INTEGRITY SYSTEM

10 On-Going Reforms Relevant to Curbing Corruption: The Contribution of Decentralisation

F.X.K. Lubanga

Introduction

The Local Government Reform Programme in Uganda is officially referred to as decentralisation. It is a reform measure that affects all aspects of governance. It transferred (devolved) authority across sectors to elected local governments. Its major features are the vertical transfer of financial and personnel control to local governments, and the increase in the latitude of autonomous decision-making powers of local councils. It has caused the creation of new institutions, procedures and practices. It has therefore caused a systemic change. Since the reform not only transfers resources to local government but also transfers the authority to allocate the resources and exercise discretionary power, it has the potential either for reducing corruption or for exacerbating it.

This short paper discusses the contribution which the implementation process of the decentralisation programme has made to curbing corruption at the centre and the institutional and procedural changes that have been introduced at the local level to reduce instances of corruption, and the systems being introduced to make it difficult for officials to indulge in corrupt practices with impunity. It also examines a number of actions that must be taken to give the decentralisation process greater potency in curbing corruption.

The contribution of the local government reform programme in curbing corruption

Corruption, according to D. Kato, can in a general sense be defined as any practice or act or omission by a public official or private individual or company which violates or deviates from the laid down or generally accepted norms, rules, procedures and principles governing the expected performance of official duties with the intention or expectation of personal or group gain or advantage. It may take the form of embezzlement, bribery, patronage, leaking vital information to a competing party, over or underinvoicing, nepotism and other manifestations of abuse of office.[1]

The contribution to be made by the local government reform programme in curbing corruption may be explained by the objectives government hopes to achieve through the policy of decentralisation. The objectives are to:

- transfer real power to districts and thus reduce the load of work on remote and under-resourced central officials;
- bring political and administrative control over services to the point where they are actually delivered, thereby improving accountability and effectiveness, and promoting people's feeling of ownership of programmes and projects executed in their districts;
- free local managers from central constraints and, as a long-term goal, allow them to develop organisational structures tailored to local circumstances; and
- improve financial accountability and responsibility by establishing a clear link between the payment of taxes and the provision of services they finance.

The objectives address three main areas:

(a) political: to democratise local governments, to empower the people and promote local participation, to encourage participation of interest groups outside the government system, to promote political accountability and reduce inter and intra-district lopsided allocation of resources.

(b) organisational/managerial: to build capacity at the local level, to rationalise and reorganise the civil service to promote efficiency and effectiveness, and to enhance transparency and accountability.

(c) economic: to enhance local absorptive capacity, to increase local resource mobilisation, to introduce local choice in priority setting, to reduce the dependency syndrome and promote the spirit of self-help.

The local government reform has contributed in curbing corruption through the systemic and procedural changes that have been introduced. They are described below:

Before decentralisation financial transfers to districts were determined by each line ministry responsible for a sector. What each district office received was at the whims of ministry officials. Sums dispatched tended to reflect the negotiating powers of the local officials and the subjective consideration of senior officials at a ministry headquarters. Measures introduced under financial decentralisation have introduced two important changes. First central government allocations to local governments (inter-governmental transfers) are governed by objective criteria. Second, funds for local government operations are no longer routed through line ministries. Instead, the Ministry of Finance remits funds directly to the Accounting Officer of a district. The remittance of money directly to districts under district votes instead of routing it through ministry headquarters has eliminated "leakages" between MFEP– line ministries and districts. Ghost employees have been spotted and eliminated. For example, when districts in batch 2 (the 14 districts in the second phase of decentralisation) assumed responsibility for the payroll a total of UShs: 381,092,640 was saved. Of this UShs 192,092,640 was returned to the Treasury.[2]

Before decentralisation, nearly all local governments spent money without approved budgets. The budget and expenditure process was known only to a few. Without an approved budget, expenditures are unauthorised, and no budget performance evaluation can be undertaken. Since the start of the financial decentralisation process, all councils have been required to approve their budgets as a first step towards making the budget management process transparent. It also makes it possible for the district officials to use the budget as a tool of management. Insistence on having budgets drawn up and approved has enabled all parties, namely councillors, Local Government-appointed officials and the centre (Ministries of Finance, Local Government, and so on) to have a full picture of what had been approved and therefore be able to monitor and evaluate the budgetary and financial management performance of local governments.

New budget procedures have been introduced to help make the process even more transparent. The new budget cycle has been devised to promote accountability and transparency. The process also reduces opportunities for skewed intra-district resources allocation. In addition to this, many districts whose management capacities are above average have implemented the requirement that the full Council must be presented with costed quarterly action plans, sector by sector, at the beginning of each quarter and a quarterly report in respect of the preceding quarter.

New institutions to carry out financial auditing, and to promote compliance with rules and regulations of financial management and control have been created as part and parcel of institutional overhaul following decentralisation. The Internal Audit, Local Government Accounts Committees (local equivalents of Public Accounts Committee (PAC)) and the Auditor General have been given a greater role to bring about greater accountability. New institutions will be helpful only if officers do not collude with auditors and suppliers of goods and services.

The requirement for each local government to prepare financial statements, especially Final Accounts, has helped reduce instances of intractable embezzlement and misappropriation. If the accounts are examined expeditiously by the Auditor -General, the Local Government Accounts Committees (local Public Accounts Committees) will be in a position to recommend punitive measures for any corrupt omissions or commission. Before decentralisation, the Public Accounts Committee (PAC), on account of its busy schedule, used to handle reports of the Auditor-General on local governments three or four years in arrears. Belated action by PAC never had the deterrent and instructive effect which it should otherwise have had.

Prior to the implementation of decentralisation, the Public Service Commission used to take ages before effecting the appointment of local government officials. This offered a golden opportunity to the Chief Executives of local governments to make a large number of temporary appointments. Over time, such appointments became the fast lane for the appointment of people not qualified for the posts. Where such people met the minimum qualifications, resort to temporary appointments denied other applicants equal opportunities to be interviewed in a competitive setting since those offered temporary appointments were subsequently offered probationary and, eventually, permanent and pensionable appointments. The creation of District Service Committees and their investiture with authority to handle conclusively all matters relating to appointment, discipline and dismissal has helped reduce instances of irregular appointments.

Actions that should be taken to increase the impact of decentralisation on curbing corruption

Line ministries should increase their capacity for support supervision and bring to prominence their quality assurance roles.

The Inspector General of Government (IGG) should increase his outreach role to "test-check" for corrupt practices on surprise missions and promptly bring the offenders to book in a publicised manner so that his actions acquire a deterrent as well as a punitive character. Articles 230 and 232 (c) of the Constitution should be applied to increase the effective arm-reach of the IGG within the context of decentralisation.

Many upright council officials get caught in the web of corrupt tenderers because they lack knowledge in tendering procedures and contract management. Training sessions in methods of contracting out, evaluation of bids, contract negotiation and supervision of contractors should be conducted to ensure value for money. Line ministries and the Central Tender Board should circulate from time to time comparative prices (ranges of prices) for goods and services and normal input standards/quantities for engineering (public) works. This would help members of Local Tender Boards in making good judgements when considering tender bids, and so on.

Designing ex-ante and ex-poste monitoring evaluation systems by each line ministry as part of the introduction of Monitoring and Evaluation Systems would help in making the process of accountability more practical and exacting. Introduction of Annual Evaluation Boards—similar to annual surveys of stores and cash – to contrast what has been done with what a local government set out to do at the beginning of a financial year and holding this picture against the financial and human resources deployed would be helpful. This would compel officials to be cost -conscious and results-oriented. It would be useful to publish the findings. This would promote accountability if the general public is informed through *barazas* (public meetings) and other media about the findings. The public and organisations of civil society would be availed the "ammunition" to censure the elected officials of local governments and eventually hold them on a "short leash."

Under the existing institutional arrangements, there is no institution or person who can stop a local government official from perpetrating an unlawful action that is not of a criminal nature. Some Councils (a handful though) have continued to spend funds in the first four months of each financial year without authority; others have attempted to usurp powers of District Service Commissions to hire and fire local government employees; others have defied the law requiring the City Council to allocate 50% of the revenue they collect to Division Councils using objective criteria. Matters would be helped a lot if the IGG was granted authority by law to have a *locus standi* to move court to make declaratory judgements against local governments which infringe the law by omission or commission.

Conclusion

The decentralisation process has already made a major contribution towards curbing corruption. As the awareness of the general public is raised over their civic rights and the power of their vote, instances of undetected and unpunished corrupt practices will be on the decline. However, too much confidence should not be placed on public awareness and civil society. The watchdog institutions of the IGG, the Auditor-General and the Police must continue to raise their performance profile. Otherwise, no political grouping – central or local – has a monopoly of virtue; just as none has a monopoly of vice. Institutional checks and balances, and networking therefore remain important. Above all, prompt and effective sanctions must be applied against errant council officials to demonstrate that one cannot indulge in corrupt practices with impunity.

11 Capacity-Building with Results-Orientation and Integrity in Mind: The Experience Of Uganda

Mohammad A. M. Kisubi

Uganda is the trend-setter in Africa in the process of reforming government, attacking corruption and focusing on service delivery and results orientation. This paper discusses how the government of Uganda developed its approach which has been fundamental to defusing centralised corruption and enhancing results-orientation. The civil service is currently being transformed into a 'public' service, through decentralisation, whose purpose derives from the needs of the public being served, and one which is measured by the impact of this approach on the service delivery outputs and outcomes.

A. Decentralisation with results-orientation and empowering citizens

In 1992, Uganda embarked on a comprehensive Civil Service Reform programme that reviewed and rationalised government ministries and departments, both in structures, numbers of staff and functions. This culminated in the reduction of staff numbers from 320,000 in 1992 to well below 140,000 by December 1994. The government ministries were reduced from 35 to 21 and management of government parastatals has been either divested, privatised or commercialised. This has resulted in more efficiency and effectiveness and reduction in procedures, bureaucracy and red tape. The government remained with those functions that it could afford to run based on results-oriented management and value for money, and the rest were divested to the private sector. This has marked a change whereby most Ugandans looked at the public sector as the main employer. More and more private enterprises are springing up and more employment opportunities and competition for better quality heightened.

Uganda, since 1993, has also embarked on another reform process of decentralisation under which districts have been invested with new mandates, new resources and responsibilities for the management, administration and provision of such fundamental services as education, health, water and roads. Through the passage of the Local Government Statute and the new Constitution, Uganda has dramatically changed the framework within which local governments operate.

Essentially, districts have now more power, more resources, responsibilities and decision-making autonomy than under the old centralised system. Their performance will thus be increasingly important for growth, poverty alleviation and long-term development prospects. Thirty-nine decentralised districts and their municipalities are busy trying to develop capabilities to perform effectively in the new duties. As a result, a natural concern has emerged within Uganda on the capacity of local governments and the appropriate means of strengthening it.

Positive outcomes in the decentralisation reform process

Local governance and political reforms

The political environment within which local governments operate has experienced significant changes. The local district leaders and councillors at various levels have been popularly elected. The selection of such persons is more transparent and fair. The citizens' participation has been enhanced to the extent that they can now question the performance of their leaders and even recall them. Local government accountability has been enhanced.

A reduction in the central government presence and an introduction of the local council system right from the village level, has introduced more transparent and fair electoral practices. These have in turn, conferred more legitimacy on the leadership role of district local council chairpersons in the public's eye and made the position of the District Local Council Chairman more attractive and competitive. An important result has been a change in the nature of district leadership. Formerly, district managers were 'outsiders' posted by the central government. Now, with decentralisation, district political life has become clearly more local in nature, increasing demands on new leaders to respond to their communities.

Experience at the local district scene indicates that competition for political office has, in many cases, opened the doors to responsible, more transparent, more accountable and more innovative local leadership. This, in turn, has become the driving force behind capacity building efforts. More widespread community participation and growing civic involvement have expanded the range of possibilities open to districts and provided the basis to sustain the local government capacity over time.

Mobilisation and utilisation of resources

Since the beginning of decentralisation, districts have experienced a sharp increase in available resources. Districts now have the impetus to raise more and more local resources as they retain most of the resources at the different collection pints. Some of the districts have made significant efforts in mobilising local resources and this is reflected in the expansion in service coverage and quality. This is very promising in that the districts are now in a better position to undertake and sustain local development initiatives. There is also a five-year capacity building plan to ensure that the districts are assisted and facilitated to acquire the necessary qualified and experienced personnel, logistics and equipment and systems in place to ensure successful implementation of the decentralization process.

Active community participation and direct involvement

Community participation is enforcing local government accountability. At the same time it is broadening the resources which the district administration could draw upon to improve its capacity. Decentralisation has been welcomed by most Ugandans who nostalgically longed for the good old days enjoyed in the 1960s when everyone did certain jobs like maintaining feeder roads, digging wells and protecting springs, etc. not for pay but for '*Bulungi Bwansi*', i.e. for the good of my country. What used to happen in those days is that on a particular day, a representative of the village chief would sound a drum and, depending on the need, everyone would assemble either to clear a road, improve on the water system or undertake any activity in a communal manner.

The centralisation of powers had made people to abandon their ways of self-help and be dependent on central government to do everything including employing people to dig their own feeder roads. The result over time has been dependence on higher authorities, hence the feeling of helplessness. The 'Bulungi Bwansi' tradition, on which most of Ugandans' cultural values are based, is being awakened by decentralisation. This is one of the immediate success stories of decentralisation: The realisation that the citizens do not have to wait for central government to give them services and provide all the infrastructure. They now realize the central government cannot provide everything. They are now holding discussions as to what central government should do and what they can do as a community for their own well-being. This has created a sense of responsibility and an opportunity to reactivate the *'Bulungi Bwansi'* tradition of communal work.

The local committees are forming clubs of togetherness, where each person who becomes a member contributes something every month or so in a village kind of bank and is able to draw reasonable funds to kick-start income-generating activities or clearing land and planting crops which he would sell after a few months, pay back the loan and save something for himself/herself. It is this kind of growth that can be sustained over time and give the right impetus and encouragement from central government . It can also be one way of fighting and eradicating poverty of the rural poor who make up over 90% of Uganda's population. This is what decentralisation is doing well for the people, taking services and opportunities nearer to the people; empowering them and making them responsible for their own services and well-being.

The practice of communities being involved in deciding their priorities and contributing labour and materials for public programs and projects is increasing not only the available resources but also cost -effectiveness and user satisfaction.

Voice of the citizens

Due to the decentralisation process the citizens are now having a voice. The consistent expression of community demands an important factor explaining the development of local government capacity. The voice of the citizens has made local authorities more accountable and more responsible to the citizens, increasing the political costs of inefficient and inadequate public decisions. As a result, it is making local governments more interested in changing their administrations and personnel to make them more effective. In several cases, protests and civic mobilisations are forcing local governments to make decisions and take action in favor of the citizens. This way, the community voice is performing as a way of enhancing local government capacity.

Ensuring sustainable capacity development

A majority of the local governments are giving attention to areas such as staff skills and professionalisation, equipment, materials and buildings, organisation, planning and execution functions. This they are doing by drawing upon the resources which already existed inside the public sector or in the community that were not fully utilised under the old system. They have also initiated efforts to upgrade the skills of their staff (through new hiring and training), expand the equipment available to them (for example, contracting out to the private sector), and improve the way local administrations work (for example, involving users in decision-making). The above illustrate that decentralisation, if properly steered, can succeed and the capacity of local governments can be enhanced through skilful innovations even under difficult circumstances, given the right political incentives and if the community and its leadership are determined.

All districts have vigorously embarked on the attractions and recruitment of well-qualified and experienced personnel. This is a contrast to the hitherto practice of receiving staff from the center whether they are effective or not and whether they have the district at heart or not. However, capacity enhancement requires local governments to undertake reforms in the way they conduct their operations, to make investments in human resources and equipment, to adopt new work practices.

The local leadership is also showing control over the staff working in the districts, especially with regard to their performance and behaviour, something unknown in the past, where badly behaved or inefficient staff were merely transferred from one district to another without proper disciplinary action or mechanisms. Districts now have powers to deal with corruptive tendencies and abuse of office. This was impossible under the central government. The best that could have been done would have been transfer of the official to another station. Decentralisation has increased responsibility and discipline among staff.

Reforming management systems, planning and execution processes

Good people working for a badly organised district administration, or without the necessary management tools, will not go far in terms of effectiveness. New responsibilities make it imperative for the districts to undertake some type of administrative reforms: changing the structure of the district administration organisation, creating new or merging departments, establishing the corresponding division of responsibilities and channels of communication.

Regarding the execution of programmes, the experience here indicates some weaknesses. It is at the level of implementing programmes that many districts face capacity limitations. Capacity in this area seems to be closely associated with various other dimensions such as strong leadership, community involvement in programmes, clear priorities, and an effective district organisation.

Cost sharing

Another area which is working because of decentralisation but had failed as a central government policy is that of cost-sharing in hospitals and health centers. The districts, because of the special powers given to them by the Decentralisation Statute, have been able to convince people to engage in cost-sharing so as to improve the quality of services in the health sector. The people are willingly contributing because they demand to see the direct connection between what they are paying and the drugs, feeding of patients, bedding, etc. in the health units, for example. In fact, they have gone beyond cost-sharing and in some cases provided housing and food to the staff in the health units. This too is a motivating factor to the health staff who now see themselves as part of the local community. This has been heightened further by the formation of health units management committees (HUMCs) to manage and deal with all issues pertaining to the health units. The committees are composed of members of the local community and those from the health units. These committees have been instrumental in the expansion of coverage and improvement on health services delivery. An important example of this great partnership is exhibited where the health staff agree with the local populace as to what time of the week is best suited for immunisation; that is, when the mothers are free. This has ensured that immunisation of all children is undertaken at the pace and agreement of the mothers. It is this kind of approach that is bringing people into the management of their affairs and destiny.

District associations

Co-operative forms of association between districts can play an important role in the capacity building of local administrations. Decentralisation has brought about inter-district co-operation, unknown in the past where there was no centre in district relationships. Neighbouring districts knew nothing about one another and could not help one another without first going to the centre. Now districts can even choose to collaborate in offering services, hire out joint services, etc. to accrue from economies of scale. For instance, districts are collaborating in hiring road construction services rather than each trying on their own to do simple road maintenance. Also district reports inform each other of companies that do shoddy work so that they are not hired.

Another important thing is that decentralisation will help to check the movement of dubious officers from one district to another. If an officer embezzles or steals in one district he will find it hard to be employed in another district because of the strong inter-district links and collaboration. District officials are also visiting one another (kind of study tours) so that they can learn from each other and share experiences. This is particularly helping the less successful districts to emulate the more successful ones, leading to an all win-win situation.

Involving the private sector

An important aspect of capacity development is for local governments to learn how to work with new partners that can significantly expand their capacity to perform their responsibilities and provide services to their population. Practically all districts have private contractors to execute part of their construction projects. Beyond that, the evidence on collaboration between the public and private sectors at the local level is still scarce. The privatisation of services does not appear prominently in the agenda of most local governments. There is ample room to advance local capacity by involving the private sector. An example could be to contract private health personnel to give support supervision to those in government facilities or even contract them to give specialised services like dental, etc.

The challenge ahead

It is evident that since 1993, Uganda has embarked on a process of decentralisation which, combined with other structural reforms, is reshaping, in a fundamental manner, the way public policies are conducted. However, the transition to this new system is not an easy one. Yet, against all odds, the picture on the decentralisation process emerging from the districts is encouraging. There is evidence of increased service coverage, citizen satisfaction, attention to rural areas and women, children and the poor, cost-consciousness and resource mobilisation efforts.

However, it is not all rosy with the decentralisation process. Decentralisation experience has been marked by ups and downs. This should not be seen as a failure but rather as an opportunity to strengthen it further. Because, just like a child beginning to walk cannot be expected to begin running, it should rather be encouraged to stand up whenever it falls. Equally districts need guidance, assistance and, most important, encouragement if we are to see development and growth in the districts. And just like kids even of the same age master walking at a different pace and time, so will districts be in their development strategies. Some are making very steady progress while others seem to be making progress or none at all. Although decentralisation does not come with answers, Uganda's experience shows that it nevertheless tries to answer and respond to what people really need. The challenge is up to the government to make periodic assessments on a district-by-district basis and follow up the implementation process to ensure that all districts are helped to realise the aims and objectives of decentralisation.

The districts need constructive guidance and assistance. The challenge is to make the environment conducive for the emergence and consolidation of a system in which multiple agents (public and private) are positioned to offer support to local governments. The role of the central ministries and departments would be more sharply focused on developing ways to leverage incentives already being felt in civil society. National authorities at the centre would thus become enablers of possibilities, rather than direct executioners or builders of district institutional strength. Therefore ministries and the centre should become partners and enablers of efforts conducted at the local level.

Decentralization requires joint effort of different actors at the local scene. In this approach, the many civil society actors, public and private, national, regional and local actors become the agents of change.

The issue of corruption and integrity in Decentralisation

Since the beginning of decentralisation, districts have experienced a sharp increase in available resources. Districts now have the impetus to raise more and more local resources as they retain most of the resources at the different collection points. Districts also have access to additional resources from the national level, either as Block Grants or Equalisation Grants. For the first time, districts also have access to credit. Under the new system, districts assume key responsibilities for the provision of services and the execution of public expenditure programmes. Among the responsibilities are the development and maintenance of the infrastructure, provision and extension of services, the mobilisation of resources, the provision of basic water and sanitation, the promotion of rural development, and the maintenance of law and order at local level.

The question here is whether the new district administrators and managers and political leaders will not squander the resources and be corrupted by the system. This is where all Ugandans need to come in and educate the citizens how to detect corrupt tendencies and expose corrupt practices among the society in which they live. Indeed, the act of taking services nearer to the people will improve transparency and accountability. Hence decentralisation could be a way of combating corruption. But this requires that the general public is involved and participates in decision making and insisting on accountability and transparency. Thus, corruption must be rooted out for a national integrity system to thrive.

Political reforms

The political environment within which local governments operate is also an important step towards a good national integrity system. Corrupt and untrustworthy leaders tend to corrupt the public and the entire system. It is not surprising that during our years of turmoil and uncertainty, people simply resorted to taking what was possible as fast as possible for they knew not what would happen tomorrow. This has now changed. The local district leaders and councillors at various levels have been popularly elected. The selection of such persons is more transparent and fair. The citizens' participation has been enhanced to the extent that they can now question the performance of their leaders and even recall them. Local government accountability has been enhanced. However, the new arrangements are not fully operative. Different levels of local district administrations need time to understand and adapt to the new modus operandi.

Service delivery surveys and citizen satisfaction

Building a national integrity system will not have succeeded if the citizens do not get satisfied with the services rendered by their respective local administrations and rights upheld and law and order maintained. Thus a key element in the assessment of a national integrity system's that effectiveness should be associated with the views expressed by the citizens. Service delivery surveys and mechanisms of monitoring citizen satisfaction should be instituted. This will help in giving service as required, ensuring quality and satisfaction. Most of the citizens thus tend to favour and trust the local authorities more than the national ones in the provision of services. Also there is greater increased community participation and contributions in labor, materials and even money.

The role of the Press

The press can do a good job by educating the public and civil society that mere amassing of property is not a measure of success. This could be done by exposing many of the people who have acquired properties through illegal and corrupt ways. When such people are put in courts and punished, the public will begin to see and treat them differently. The press should also help to educate and inform the public about their rights and duties. No national integrity system can function without the different parts in that system knowing who does what and why. It is only through such information that citizens will be expected to play their rightful roles and be able to demand what is due to them.

Exposure of corrupt tendencies should be made and those concerned punished so as to bring sanity back in society. The whistle-blowers in civil society on corrupt practices and people must be guaranteed protection and confidentiality. Complaints offices should also be opened up where aggrieved people could lodge complaints for a follow-up. Newspapers could also have columns for the public to make complaints and seek reactions.

The role of religions and education

Religious institutions and religious leaders have a lot of audience and fora which can be used to preach and counsel their followers about evils in society and bad behaviour, immorality, corruption, etc. They should make good morality, integrity, accountability and transparency preaching. This is one sure way of rebuilding and sustaining an integrity system. School administrators and teachers have a part and parcel of their important role to play by educating the young generation about good morals, behaviour expected of good citizens, roles and duties of citizens and the dangers of corruption.

The challenge for the Civil Society

While signs of a good national integrity system are beginning to appear, the process may be impeded by doubt, uncertainty, and even strained relations among the different players in the civil society. A legacy of antagonism, don't care attitude, a sense of irresponsibility, non-accountability and lack of transparency developed over time may creep in to derail the process. These carry mixed messages of freedom floating in an atmosphere of doubt and new obligations. The evidence however suggests that many Ugandans are fed up with the way and manner in which they have been living and for once they are asserting their rights and defending their interests. It is high time that Ugandans strived to develop a good national integrity system.

C. Transparency Uganda: A Citizens' organization to fight corruption

Issues of transparency and accountability have become increasingly important in the post-Cold War world. In recipient countries, like Uganda, the movement towards decentralization, public sector reforms, privatisation and commercialisation of many government functions has increased the range of opportunities available to citizens and brought demands for greater responsiveness on the part of government and parastatal agencies. In an era of dwindling aid budgets and a skeptical public, donors are now seeking better value for their money. They are less willing to excuse widespread graft and corruption. Donors are increasingly recognising that lack of transparency, corrupt project management, and poor accountability are major obstacles to effective implementation of donor-funded projects. Increasingly, multi and bilateral donors are dealing explicitly with these issues in their declamatory policy and in the design of its projects.

Fighting corruption cannot be left to one institution alone. The public and the private sectors, religious organisations, and all groups of goodwill ought to be involved. It is in this light that Transparency Uganda was formed in 1995. This organisation is affiliated with Transparency International (TI) which is an international non-governmental organisation based in Germany. Its international mandate is to counter corruption in international business. TI has many national chapters which are steadily increasing; Transparency Uganda being one of the latest.

Transparency Uganda regards corruption as the number one enemy to economic development and social justice. Its existence and proliferation impair and impede smooth delivery of public services and derail government projects and programmes. Corruption dehumanises public officials and diverts national resources from public to private or personal ends. It distorts the economy.

For the fight against corruption to succeed it must be grounded on a firm political commitment which will provide a conducive atmosphere for the enforcement of the laws without fear, favour or discrimination. Transparency Uganda also believes that, for the fight against corruption to be successful, it must involve all sections of the civil society. Individual and collective efforts are needed in an endeavour to create national values that will promote transparency, accountability and good governance.

But, whereas the other institutions belong more or less to government, Transparency Uganda is an independent organisation and more representative of the civil society which may be relied on to play the role of whistle-blowing, public awareness and a venue through which the public can direct complaints to government institutions. It is in this light that Transparency Uganda has embarked on the establishment of a Secretariat with an office and a small staff. In the long run, the organisation will work towards the establishment of a Secretariat with an office and a new staff. In the long run Transparency Uganda will work towards establishing a fully fledged office with its own premises and logistics.

In this respect, it intends to educate the public through the media, pamphlets, conduct seminars and meetings, promote drama activities and carry out shows through television. This will equip the general public with the necessary information about the trend of corruption in Uganda and amplify the role the public can and has to play in the fight against corruption.

Part Five

ROLE OF THE ENFORCEMENT AGENCIES

12 The Director of Public Prosecutions and Crime Prevention

Alfred P.W. Nasaba

Introduction

The effective control of crime and protection of citizens are at the heart of government responsibility. If a nation cannot meet this basic responsibility, it has little hope of realising its social, economic and cultural potential. Crime is a particularly serious impediment to harmonious development. It dissipates or misdirects the gains of economic growth and degrades the quality of life.

Serious crime is an exceptionally severe problem in a majority of the nations. Crime within national borders is only part of the problem. Over the past several years, transnational crime has accelerated to scarcely believable dimensions. Modern means of communication, travel, and transfer of goods and money have turned domestic criminal enterprises into international threats.

In Uganda, there is a general outcry among the populace because of the excessively long period it takes for criminal cases to be disposed of while suspects languish in prisons awaiting trial. There are many causes that give rise to such delays and they are generally attributed to the Judiciary, the police, the office of the Director of Public Prosecutions (DPP) and the prisons, which are the agencies involved in the administration of criminal justice. It is therefore the purpose of this paper to examine such underlying causes, with a view to their elimination in order to minimise perpetual denial of justice to people.

Director of Public Prosecutions

The office of the DPP was set up under Article 71 of the 1967 Uganda Constitution. Its main function is to institute and control all criminal proceedings in the country. It therefore maintains contact with other government departments and regulatory bodies such as police, prisons, judiciary, probation, financial institutions, and so on.

The aims of the department are to:

(a) Increase the efficiency of criminal justice in the country by appropriate direction of successful investigation and prosecution of criminal cases;
(b) Deter crime and maintain confidence in Uganda's criminal justice system.

In order to achieve the above aims, the objectives of the department are to pursue appropriate and prompt investigation of criminal cases and complaints, and to prosecute criminal suspects. It will ensure more effective prosecutions and consider any lessons to be learned where a prosecution results in an acquittal. The DPP will collaborate with other institutions involved in identifying, investigating, and prosecuting criminal cases. The DPP will ensure that its operations are properly reported in accordance with the above aims. He will put the department's resources to maximum effect in the direction of criminal investigations and prosecution. By stages, the DPP will implement an information systems strategy able to support the department's operations and administrations. Also, personnel management systems which provide the necessary staff resources and individual career development will be developed.

Functions

To achieve the above objectives, the department is constitutionally empowered to do the following:

(a) Institute and undertake criminal proceedings against any person or authority before any court, other than a court martial, in respect of any offences alleged to have been committed;
(b) Take over and continue any such criminal proceedings that have been instituted or undertaken by any other person;
(c) Discontinue at any stage before judgement is delivered any such criminal proceedings instituted or undertaken by any other person or authority;
(d) Give advice and directions to Criminal Investigation Department (CID) in particular and other government departments on the conduct of criminal investigations and on decisions to prosecute and on what charges;

(e) Appeal in cases where an accused is acquitted by courts if such an acquittal is erroneous in law;
(f) Give views in cases undergoing revision by the high court before revisional orders are made;
(g) Consent to charges requiring consent to prosecute, for example, sedition, corruption, abuse of office, and so on;
(h) Enter *nolle prosequi* in cases before the high court as means of withdrawing charges;
(i) Prosecute all cases, appeals, criminal revisions, and miscellaneous applications before high court and supreme court; and
(j) Appoint public prosecutors to prosecute on his behalf.

Delegation of Powers

Under Article 120 (4) of the 1995 Uganda constitution, the DPP is empowered to exercise his powers in person or through officers authorised in that behalf by him acting in accordance with his general or special instructions. In this regard, it is in fact his public prosecutors (mainly police prosecutors) and state attorneys who handle the bulk of his workload but under his control and direction. It is for that reason that there is a great need for supervision and control of the activities of the department. In order to do that, it was necessary to restructure the administrative set up of the department.

The new organisational structure

The department has been divided and is being run according to the following divisions: the Administration Division, the Inspectorate and Research Division, the General Case Work Division, the Prosecution Division, and the International and Training Division.

Relations with the Police

In order to carry out his constitutional functions, the DPP needs to have machinery for detection and investigation of crime, the processing and assembling of evidence, and the prosecution of offenders. The DPP largely relies on the police force, especially the CID and the Traffic Branch, to carry out these functions. There exists, therefore, very close collaboration between the office of the DPP and the CID in particular and the entire police in general.

Relations with the Judiciary

The relationship between the DPP and the Judiciary is very strong because the two are partners in the administration of criminal justice. They are partners in the sense that their functions are complementary. A prosecution service is therefore dependent on courts to try cases and to issue out witness summonses and arrest warrants.

The current practice is that it is the duty of the courts to pay witness expenses for witnesses summoned by the prosecution and the defence. The courts have, however, failed to execute this role. The result is that many potential witnesses these days simply refuse to come to court. Because of this, many cases are lost or dismissed in the end. It is the prosecution who are normally to blame, which seems unfair because the fault does not lie with the prosecution but with the court which has persistently failed to pay witnesses' expenses. It is therefore envisaged that in future the prosecution, which needs witnesses to prove its case, should shoulder the responsibilities to pay their expenses. In this regard, the liaison office will be responsible for co-ordinating such services.

The main function of the liaison office will be to liaison with other institutions involved in identification, investigation, prosecution, and determination of criminal cases and correctional authorities.

It is intended that such an office be headed by a uniformed police officer of and above the rank of Assistant Superintendent and a support staff of three junior officers. Among other duties, they will act as process servers and court orderlies for the prosecution whenever we have high court sessions in Kampala.

Inspectorate and Research Division

The Department of Public Prosecutions is presently the biggest department in the Attorney General's chambers. It is an expanding one with about 20 up-country offices of Resident State Attorneys. Its professional responsibilities are on the increase given that there are plans to replace police prosecutors with lay prosecutors, all of who would be directly under the control and supervision of the DPP. This therefore has necessitated the establishment of an inspectorate and research division whose functions are to:

(a) handle complaints from members of the public, police and advocates;
(b) carry out regular inspections of Resident State Attorneys and lay prosecutors;

(c) compile data of all cases received and handled in the department on a monthly basis;
(d) ensure that the DPP's operations are properly reported in accordance with the department's aims.
(e) initiate research into the current laws relating to the administration of criminal justice and to suggest necessary reforms and amendments; and
(f) liaise with other institutions involved in the administration of criminal justice.

The main function of this division is to give advice and directions to CID in particular and other government departments on the conduct of criminal investigations or on decisions to prosecute and on what charges to lay. In addition, it carries out research on relevant laws and suggests necessary assignments.

Prosecution Division

In order to ensure uniformity in prosecution where prosecution should only be carried out if the evidence provides a reasonable prospect of securing a conviction and or if it is in the public interest to bring criminal proceedings, there was need to establish a prosecution division. The functions of this division are to:
(a) ensure more effective prosecutions and, where it results in an acquittal, to consider any lessons to be learned;
(b) collaboration with other institutions involved in identifying, investigating and prosecuting criminal cases;
(c) take over and continue any criminal proceedings instituted or undertaken by the DPP or any other person or authority;
(d) discontinue at any stage before judgement is delivered any such criminal proceedings instituted or undertaken by the DPP or any other person or authority;
(e) appeal in cases where an accused is acquitted by court if such acquittal is erroneous in law;
(f) give views in cases undergoing revision by the High Court before revisional orders are made; and
(g) prosecute offences, miscellaneous applications, committal proceedings tried by the High Court and the Supreme Court.

Anti-Corruption Section

Under the Prevention of Corruption Act (8 of 1970), the DPP is empowered to investigate cases of corruption and bribery, and to prosecute the suspects. The objective of this section is to emphasize the measures that can be taken to prevent or to minimize corruption and to suggest ways in which instances of alleged corruption can be successfully investigated and prosecuted.

(a) The preventive functions are to:
   (i) instil awareness on the evils of corruption and to change people's attitude towards corrupt practices;
   (ii) study, formulate and carry out anti-corruption campaigns;
   (iii) study and analyse management systems and administration of government departments and to identify opportunities for corruption;
   (iv) process and maintain data, statistics and records on corruption cases.

(b) The investigative functions are:
   (i) to process and study all preliminary inquiries;
   (ii) to co-ordinate investigation activities carried out by the various investigation branches.

(c) The prosecution functions are:
   (i) to study and scrutinise investigation papers before issuance of consent to prosecute;
   (ii) to prosecute corruption cases.

Fraud Section

The ease with which national boundaries can be crossed, and the extraordinary facilities available for rapid travel combine to make criminals increasingly mobile. At the same time, the complex structure of modern societies, coupled with the constant growth of international exchanges provide more and more opportunities for international crime, a phenomenon which has now reached alarming proportions in Uganda.

With technological revolution, civil and criminal matters are no longer local. When cartels are formed, products dumped, environmental niches destroyed, drugs imported, or terrorists strike, the effects are no longer merely local but, rather, cross international borders.

Technological improvements in communication and information systems have made it possible to trade in securities markets throughout the world and around the clock. These changes have brought with them a number of advantages, including a broader capital base and more efficient markets. The globalisation of corporate finance has also led to a dramatic increase in the sophistication of investors who look to international markets in order to obtain greater diversification for their portfolios.

They have brought with them a number of not so happy side effects. It has become increasingly difficult to regulate trans-border trading in securities and to protect investors from international fraud. The functions of this section are thus:

(a) to explore and examine international responses to international frauds;
(b) to consider and explore ways and methods of protection against international frauds;
(c) to examine jurisdictional and constitutional problems associated with international co-operation and enforcement which can be applied to Uganda and
(d) to recommend ways and methods of fraud protection to the government for incorporation into national legislations.

International Co-operation and Training Division

International crimes and international co-operation, in the field of criminal law, are not new phenomena. But as the mobility of individuals and capital increases, so do the opportunities for international crime.

Drug trafficking, terrorism and fraud are among the many offences which cross state boundaries. Governments throughout the world are actively promoting international co-operation in response to this problem, thereby creating a new and rapidly expanding field of law. Whilst the need for such strategies may be seen as both urgent and compelling, it is clear that their adoption in the administration of our criminal justice system may have considerable implications for the rights of individuals.

Although judicial co-operation in the handling of crime has been a feature of international relations for many years, it is only in the past five to ten years that countries have sought to create formal structures permitting co-operation in the investigation and prosecution of crime and ensuring that "international" criminals can be lawfully deprived of the proceeds of their crimes, wherever those proceeds are located.

This division is therefore intended to adopt and apply modern arrangements concluded by government and operated by a new breed of "international lawyers" whose task is to assist in:

(a) the formulation of requests;
(b) ensuring that foreign requests are dealt with efficiently;
(c) having a thorough working knowledge of global co-operative regimes and national legal systems;
(d) initiating seminars and conferences to discuss issues of particular concern to those involved in combating crimes with an international dimension;
(e) providing the department with an effective and improved system for the prosecution of drug-related offences and promoting a common approach to those within the country; and
(f) studying and initiating improvements of legislation for drug offences, in line with the provisions of the 1988 Convention on Illicit Traffic in Narcotic Drugs and Psychotropic Substances and other relevant UN instruments.

Central Authority Section

For Uganda, the central authority is the Attorney-General or a person designated by him. All requests for mutual legal assistance are made and received on behalf of the central authority, that is the Attorney-General, by the DPP's department. The main functions of the Central Authority Section are to:

(a) advise the Attorney-General on matters of mutual legal assistance, for example extradition;
(b) liaise with the Attorney-General for purposes of establishing a competent central office for Uganda;
(c) initiate legislations regarding mutual legal assistance and advise the Attorney-General accordingly; and
(d) seek international assistance in the establishment of the central office in Uganda.

Resident State Attorney's Office

The DPP is housed in the parliamentary buildings at the Ministry of Justice and Constitutional Affairs headquarters. The office is a very busy one and therefore it would be plainly impossible for all the workload from all over the country to be effectively handled at the headquarters.

In this regard under Article 120 (4) of the 1995 constitution, the DPP exercises his power through officers appointed as Resident State Attorneys to man up-country stations. They act in accordance with his general or special instructions. In this regard, it is in fact the Resident State Attorneys and police prosecutors who handle the bulk of this work-load but under his control and direction.

Presently we have 20 offices of Resident State Attorneys. They include Arua, Mbarara, Jinja, Fort-Portal, Mbale, Lira, Gulu, Kabale, Masindi, Masaka, Mubende, Tororo, Mukono, Soroti, Mpigi, Luwero, Buganda Road Court, Mengo Court, Iganga, and Bushenyi.

The objective of establishing up-country offices is to take legal services nearer to the people, which in turn leads to increased efficiency of criminal justice by appropriate direction of successful investigation and prosecution of criminal cases in those areas.

Resident State Attorneys, being the DPP's representatives in the up-country stations, handle the volume of all cases from their particular areas. Where they exist, Resident State Attorneys have been mandated to take over the functions which were being handled by police officers in charge of prosecution. The current position is that all police files are expected to be looked at by a Resident State Attorney and approved before charges are registered in court. Where we do not have a Resident State Attorney, such functions are expected to be performed by the district CID officer. All fraud-related offences are supposed to be handled and prosecuted by State Attorneys.

Each State Attorney is expected to get a monthly report from the district CID officer in districts where we are not represented but which fall under his/her jurisdiction. Currently we have State Attorneys at every chief magisterial headquarters except Moroto.

Lay prosecutors

A study has already been instituted into the possibilities of training prosecutors to eventually replace police prosecutors and we are at an advanced stage. The idea has been floated and accepted in principle by our minister. We have even discussed the issue of funding with some donor countries and now we are in the process of writing a cabinet paper to government for approval before we can move.

Research

The department has embarked on research not only in areas where the present laws need amendments but also in areas where we do not have laws at all, for example, in matters of mutual legal assistance, enforcement of drug-related and juvenile related laws, and so on.

Staffing

Staffing in the department still remains a problem despite the recent salary increases for State Attorneys. This time, however, it is not because lawyers are not willing to join the departments, but it is because there are very few established posts for them. This explains why we cannot open more offices of Resident State Attorneys up-country as we may have wished to do.

As the staffing position improves, we plan, in the short run, to open up three more offices for Resident State Attorneys in Moroto, Rakai, Kasese, and Rukungiri districts. Our long-term plan is to have a Resident State Attorney in every district with lay prosecutors attached to every Grade II and Grade III Magistrates' Courts at county and sub-county levels.

Facilities

The provision of working tools has greatly improved, thanks to the British Government, who donated seven vehicles to our up-country offices and provided us with office equipment and a photocopier which has enabled us to reproduce some legislations for our lawyers.

Currently, apart from our Resident State Attorneys at Mengo, Buganda Road, Mpigi, and Luwero, the rest have official vehicles, and provisions for maintenance and fuel are being made to enable them to operate.

As a result, there is some marked improvement in our performance, and the morale of lawyers is high. We had a seminar in January 1995 for the first time in the Ministry and it was very successful. More seminars aimed at improving staff performance are in the pipeline. It is expected that the seminar will not only include State Attorneys but also all officials who are involved in the prosecution of criminal cases in Uganda.

Guidelines on the role of prosecutors

One of the most important tasks of the DPP is its review function. This means that we consider the evidence supplied by the police, and any other relevant information, and make a decision about whether or not the case should be taken to court. We also advise the police about the strength of the evidence against the suspect or if the public interest requires a prosecution. At all times we exercise an independent judgement about the case presented to us.

The decision to prosecute an individual is a serious step. Fair and effective prosecution is essential to the maintenance of law and order. Even in a small case, a prosecution has serious implications for all involved, namely, the victim, a witness and an accused.

It is therefore important that the DPP in Uganda should, like in many other countries in the developed world, not only have guidelines on the role of prosecutions but also a code of conduct for prosecutors. Such a code would enable the prosecution service to make fair and consistent decisions. It would also help the prosecution service to play its part in making sure justice is served. It would provide State Attorneys and other officers engaged in law enforcement with clear guidelines for making decisions which arise in respect of prosecutions. Lastly, it would also inform the public of the considerations upon which decisions are made.

In that regard, the DPP has embarked on the preparation of guidelines on the role of, and a code of conduct for, prosecutors. The draft guidelines together with the code are expected to be presented at our next seminar for consideration. It is hoped that when the guidelines and the code of conduct become effective, they will regulate the official conduct of all public prosecutors in this country.

The Police Force

The functions of the Uganda Police Force include the prevention and detection of crime, the apprehension of offenders, the preservation of law and order, the protection of life and property and service as a military force when called upon.

In short, the most important duty of the police force is to enforce a social contract that exists between an individual and the state; whereby the individual undertakes to abide by the laws legally enacted by legislative institutions of the country, and Government undertakes to govern in accordance with the same laws and regulations.

The philosophy of a police force

For any police force to be able to enforce the above-mentioned social contract, it must maintain a high degree of professionalism and independence. The cardinal rule that should guide its operations is that every citizen is equal before the laws of the country. No one, be it a Minister or a peasant, should be allowed to violate the law with impunity. In the recent past, the Uganda Police Force had created an image of a government agent which enforced the laws rigidly against the common people but tended to turn a blind eye whenever the same laws were violated by big officials in government.

Yet the concept of the police force is, in reality, a professional body of men and women whose role is to enforce the laws and regulations of the country with utmost impartiality. If the police force is seen to be an instrument of oppression at the service of a few highly placed people in government, it will never receive the respect a professional police force deserves. Once the police force fails to command the respect of the people it is supposed to serve, it will never be effective. The police, therefore, rely heavily on the co-operation of the general public in order to be effective. This is presently demonstrated by the introduction of community policing within our police force.

Until the advent of the NRM government, the Uganda Police Force had been used by successive politicians as a personal instrument. The force was also used as a coercive instrument to entrench themselves and harass their political opponents. There had been a lot of political interference by politicians in the operations of the police. They had gone to the extent of ordering the police to effect arrests, participate in harassing innocent citizens, release prisoners from lawful custody, direct closures of public investigations and caused transfers and dismissal of police officers who failed to toe the line, for political considerations. This type of interference has now been reduced to a minimum, and where it occurs, police officers normally resist it without serious implications on the security of their jobs.

Functional structure of the Uganda Police

Functionally the police at present is sub-divided into the Administration, the Special Branch, the Criminal Investigation Department, the Local Administration and Operations.

For the purposes of this paper, we shall concentrate on the activities of the Criminal Investigation Department, popularly referred to as CID, as far as the police force is concerned.

The Criminal Investigation Department

The Department of Criminal Investigation has its head office in Kampala just like any of the above five departments which form the police force.

The great bulk of detection, investigation, assembling of evidence and prosecution in this country falls on the CID. This is a very highly technical department of the police force; and more often than not, the efficiency of the entire force is judged by the success or failure of the CID. In order for this department to do its work, it must first of all have highly educated, well trained, experienced, disciplined and highly motivated personnel. Theirs is not a task that can just be performed by anyone. They must be dedicated men and women of high integrity and above corruption.

The CID must be well equipped in order to perform its functions properly. They must have an excellent transport and communication system to be able to respond quickly and efficiently to reports of criminal activity all over the country. They should have properly equipped offices with sufficient stationery and custody equipment to prevent loss of valuable files and exhibits or the destruction of vital evidence. However, the staff of the department at the moment are poorly educated and trained. This has led to loss of numerous cases in court when a witness discovers that the statement he is alleged to have recorded is quite different from the evidence he is giving in court. To make matters worse, just like any other civil servant, the staff of the CID are paid a miserable salary. As a result, there appears to be a lot of abuses in the department, leading to failure to investigate cases, loss of police files, loss of exhibits and several other malpractices – the end result of which is that criminals go unpunished and too much injustice is committed against society.

Prosecution

One of the very important duties of the CID is to prosecute offenders under the general superintendence and direction of the DPP.

The CID is supposed to be equipped with sufficient knowledge of law and procedures to carry out its task. The majority of police prosecutors in this country have very low educational standards and only very few have been trained in law and procedures to conduct meaningful prosecution. To minimise this problem, the police has embarked on training its officers involved in investigation and detection of crimes by organising various training seminars and courses.

Within the CID, there is a very important but often totally neglected section called the Identification Bureau. This includes the sub-sections indicated below.

The Photographic Section

This section is responsible for all aspects of police photography of prisoners, finger prints, field photography, photocopying, and document reproduction.

Identification Bureau

The Criminal Record Office is responsible for maintaining criminal records; keeping indexes of persons wanted for or suspected of crime, identifiable stolen property, stolen motor vehicles and the method index; maintaining albums, photographs, and records of criminals for inspection by witnesses in order to identify offenders; and supervising convicts.

Fingerprint Bureau (including scenes of crime)

The duties of the Bureau include the classification, filing and maintenance of finger prints; searching finger print records to trace criminal histories of persons wanted or suspected; supplying certificates of conviction to courts and prosecutors; examining articles at, or brought from, scenes of crime and identifying traces found; preparing finger prints for purposes of evidence in the courts; and instructing police officers in finger print techniques.

From available evidence, this section has been ignored and whatever few trained officers there were, have decamped. The laboratories of the section are badly lacking in equipment necessary for its highly technical work.

In the majority of cases requiring proof by only circumstantial evidence, there is little hope of proving a single case when this section is so ignored and neglected as it has been to date. It is completely short of staff in all its units. For example, in the entire police force there is only one handwriting expert who doubles as the ballistic expert. Because all questioned documents from all parts of the country have to come to him in Kampala, it takes at least one year to obtain the result of his examination. Yet no modern CID can ever hope to be effective if personnel in various branches are not properly equipped to perform their tasks.

Force Dog Section

This is another section in the CID which has been ignored over the years. This used to be a useful aid in the investigation of crime when it still had well-trained dogs and handlers. Every modern police force relies heavily on dogs in the detection of crime, such as trailing criminals, combating narcotics smuggling, and even trafficking in explosives as well as general security and night patrols of towns, streets, and so on. It is a sad commentary on the extent of the deterioration that the Uganda police had lost such an indispensable aid to human senses. However, recent information has revealed that the Police Dog Section has an ambitious programme to re-stock the section with dogs and trained handlers and that, in fact, some dogs have arrived and are on duty. This move is strongly supported as a step in the right direction.

Lack of facilities

There is an acute shortage of all sorts of equipment throughout the entire Uganda Police Force. This includes simple office equipment such as desks, chairs, cupboards, typewriters and appropriate stationery. The government has tried hard within its available means to re-equip the police with transport; but the problem is far from solved.

While a district needs five to six vehicles to be able to quickly respond to all demands on its police establishment, most districts count themselves lucky to have one police vehicle at the moment. Even with one vehicle in the district, getting the funds for fuel and maintenance becomes yet another problem.

The Uganda Police Force has virtually no communication system. The system now in use is obsolete and breaks down so often that it no longer deserves to be called a system. Many upcountry police stations and posts are neither in communication with each other nor are they in contact with police headquarters. Lack of working facilities hampers the efficiency of the force in the detection and investigation of cases. The NRM government realises that, for economic development and prosperity to be there, internal security and the rule of law must flourish. In that respect, the Uganda Police Force plays a very vital role in the maintenance of internal stability and the rule of law. The government has therefore arranged its priorities in such a way as to give the police force its due share of the national cake so that it can play its very important role by providing for all District and Regional CID officers funds for training, courses, seminars, and so on.

Relations with Government Chemists

The Government Chemist or Analyst is yet another department under the Ministry of Internal Affairs. Its responsibilities include the analyses of viscera for the prescience of poison, the identification of poisonous or dangerous drugs, the analyses of paint, metal, glass and organic substances, the identification of semen and the estimation of the content in body fluids of alcohols such as wine.

In their day-to-day operations, the police force, especially the CID, frequently comes into close contact with the Government Chemist. The CID submits to the Government Chemist all sorts of specimens relevant to on-going investigations, for example blood, suspected poisonous substances, human tissue, and so on, in cases where poisoning is suspected. The Government Chemist examines them and prepares a report on the basis of which the CID determines whether an offence has been committed or not. The function of the Government Analyst is as important to the CID as that of the Identification Bureau.

It is, however, very unfortunate that throughout the whole country in the recent past, there was only one office of the Government Analyst situated at Wandegeya in Kampala. All samples which the CID wanted analysed by the Government Analyst had to be sent from all corners of the country to Kampala for examination. The department was known to be under-staffed and too ill-equipped to handle the multitude of requests. It took at times more than one year before results were received back at the original police station.

To make matters worse, in almost every case, a constable had to be dispatched to deliver the sample and to collect it back when it was ready, at a great expense to the police. Since the police are always short of funds and transport, dispatching and collecting the samples from the Government Chemist can be unduly delayed.

On the basis of the information gathered from the Government Chemist at Wandegeya, positive steps have been taken and two regional offices have been established at Mbarara and Mbale to cater for the western and eastern parts of the country respectively. That is a step in the right direction.

Relations with Interpol and neighbouring police forces

Interpol is the International Police organisation which links up most police forces of the world in the fight against crime. With improved and modern methods of communication, organised crime moves quickly across national borders. There is, therefore, the need for the police forces all over the world to co-operate in fighting common crimes such as drug trafficking, smuggling, the tracing of criminal fugitives, among others. At the moment, this cooperation is done through Interpol, of which Uganda is a member.

The effectiveness of the branch depends largely on its ability to communicate rapidly with other branches of Interpol in other countries and with Interpol headquarters in Paris, France. In Uganda the local branch of Interpol uses an obsolete police telecommunications system whose limitations is well known. It is therefore unable to effectively communicate information relating to criminals and crimes of interest to Interpol or to neighbouring police forces.

Use and abuse of police powers

In the exercise of their functions, the police have been given wide-ranging powers under the law. The most important of these powers is the power to arrest. Everyday, hundreds of Ugandans get arrested by the police for some reason or other. In this respect, they are like any other police force all over the world and there is nothing new in carrying out arrests.

What is worrisome to us, however, is the extent to which the Uganda police abuse the powers of arrest. In many countries of the world, the police make arrests after investigations have established a prima facie case against the suspect.

In Uganda, the rule seems to be "arrest first, investigate later." As a result, the police have persistently failed to comply with the law requiring that people who are arrested should be taken to court within twenty-four hours. The major reason is that the police are unable to charge the arrested person because they are not yet sure of what charge to prefer.

Cases are very common where suspects are detained at police stations for months before they are taken to court. At times, after such a long period of detention, the suspect is released without any charges being preferred against him in court. Since many victims of this abuse of police powers are poor or ignorant people, they cannot afford to sue the government for a civil remedy. They are doomed to suffer the injustice in silence.

As noted in the first part of this paper, this problem is being seriously addressed by the offices of the DPP by requiring all new cases to be looked at and certified by the offices of Resident State Attorneys or, where State Attorneys do not exist, the district CID officer in person before cases are registered in court.

Conclusions

The community and the state bear obvious costs to fund the operation of an extensive criminal justice system comprising the police and investigators, a prosecution service, a judiciary, a system of confinement and rehabilitation programmes designed to alleviate the plight of victims and a variety of related services. The costs of these services constitute a significant proportion of the state budgets. High direct social costs stem principally from the serious drain on the human and material resources of countries, reducing the capacity of governments to meet other needs. If the state is perceived as being unable to prevent and respond adequately to crime, the confidence of citizens in the efficiency of their government is severely undermined, frustration turns to despair and then to embittered indifference, and the capacity for personal and national productivity is severely diminished.

Moreover, domestic peace and stability are threatened. Over a period of time, crime can lead a nation into one of several forms of social decline. It can result, in extreme cases, in chaos, or in government repression. Furthermore, private protection and enforcement measures often develop and surpass the limits established by law, and violent self-help (mob justice) is sometimes undertaken as a last resort.

Individuals may experience direct financial costs through medical expenses, loss of earnings and loss of property. As crime rises, the costs of those functions also rise.

Lastly, if government is unable to perform its most fundamental functions – protecting citizens from real or potential criminals – it loses public trust and confidence, which is detrimental to the preservation and promotion of law and order. Without an effective programme of crime prevention and control, no educational effort, no agricultural returns, no anti-poverty measures, no industrial programmes can really be fully successful. Without domestic tranquillity and confidence in government there can be no true social and economic evolution or attainment of postulated national goals. This therefore explains the importance of the role of the DPP and the police in the prevention of crime in this country.

References

Bayley, D.H., 'Accountability and Control of Police: Lessons for Britain' in T. Bennett (ed.), *The Future of Policing, Cambridge: Cropwood Papers,* Institute of Criminology, 1983), pp. 146-58.

——————. *Patterns of Policing: A Comparative International Analysis,* New Brunswick: Rutgers University Press, 1985.

Collin, R.O., 'The Blunt Instruments: Italy and the Police' in J. Roach and J. Thomaneck (eds.), *Police and Public Order in Europe*, London: Croomhelm, 1985, pp. 185-213.

Cold for Crown Prosecutors, June, 1994.

Constitution of Uganda, a Law of Uganda, 1967.

de Liege, M.P. The Fight Against Crime and Fear: A New Initiative in France,' in Hope and Shaw (eds.) *Communities and Crime Reduction* (London: HMSO, 1988).

Gill, M.L., and Mawby, R.I., (1990b), *Volunteers in the Criminal Justice System: A Comparative Study of Probation, Police and Victims Support,* Milton Keynes: Open University Press.

Judicature Act, Cap 34, *Laws of Uganda*, 1964.

King, M., *How to Make Social Crime Prevention Work: The French Experience,* London: NACRO, 1988.

Mawby, R.I., *Comparative Policing Issue: The British and American Experience in International Perspective* (London, Unwin Hyman, 1990).

Penal Code Act, Cap. 106, *Laws of Uganda*, 1964.

Police Statute, *Laws of Uganda*, 1994.

Prevention of Corruption Act, *Laws of Uganda*, 1970.

13 The Role of Police in Fighting Corruption

John Cossy Odomel

Introduction

Corruption shares many of the characteristics of venereal disease. Neither victims nor perpetrators want to talk about it; those who have never encountered it are afraid to discuss it in case others think they have been involved in it; and absence of debate not only does not prevent it from spreading, but actually makes it more difficult to control.

Details to elaborate the variety of conditions under which people turn to corruption will not be covered in this paper, but extensive interviews with suspects in corruption cases give the impression that corrupt people come from all walks of life and professions. Situational factors and social background may be crucial, but it is important to bear in mind that almost any civil servant, business or professional person has the knowledge and the opportunity to be corrupt once he has decided to be so. As Swift states in *Gulliver's Travels*,

"Care and vigilance, with a very common understanding, may preserve a man's goods from thieves, but honesty hath no fence against superior cunning."

Criminal records data and my own experience indicate that corruption is practised as long as the opportunity to do so presents itself. One should note, that unlike most crimes, corruption can be taken up at any time during life–we seldom observe the natural "progression" from juvenile delinquency to adult crime among people involved in the offence of corruption as such. I, however, will not just confine myself to the offence of corruption as defined in the Prevention of Corruption Act of 1970. This is because corruption in itself has always been narrowly defined under the law. Offences including Forgery, Uttering Goods and Money by False Pretences and Abuse of Office will be discussed. A critical examination of these offences exposes an element of corruption when the world "Corruption" is used loosely and not in the legal sense.

The criminal law and corruption

In a wider sense, most members casually use the word "corruption" when referring to the use of one's official position to achieve personal gains. On the other hand, the Prevention of Corruption Act No. 8 of 1970 defines the offence of corruption as follows:

> Section 1. Any person who shall, by himself or in conjunction with any other person,
>
> (a) Corruptly solicit or receive, or agree to receive for himself, or for any other person; or
>
> (b) Corruptly give, promise or offer to any person whether for the benefit of that person or of another person,
>
> Any gratification as an inducement to or reward for, or otherwise on account of any member, officer or servant of a public body doing or forbearing to do anything in respect of any matter or transaction whatsoever, actual or proposed, in which the said public body is concerned, shall be guilty of an offence.

Section 4 of the Act deals with bribery of a member of a public body. A person convicted of an offence under Section 1, 2, 3, or 4 of the Act is liable, on conviction, to imprisonment for up to 10 years or to a fine not exceeding twenty thousand shillings or to both. An aggravating circumstance is provided for in Section 5(2); where a person "has been found guilty of corruption, the sentence may go up to 12 years' imprisonment or a fine of up to forty thousand shillings or both if the matter or transaction in relation to which the offence was committed was a contract or a proposal for a contract with a public body".

The Director of Public Prosecutions (DPP) has power to authorise a police officer not below the rank of Assistant Superintendent of Police to seize any documents in possession of the suspect or his wife or child or his trustee or agent if he considers that these documents can provide evidence of the commission of an offence under the Act (Section 13). Most unfortunately, Section 27A of the repealed Police Act was not included in the new Police Statute. This section gave special powers to the police in the investigation of crime. We are now left with Section 7 of the Evidence (Bankers' Books) Act which empowers a court to authorise the police to have access to bank accounts of a suspect. This order, however, can only be obtained compulsorily after arrest or the issue of a summons. Except for terrorism, the need to widen powers is greater in corruption cases than for any other area of crime. This is because the "giver" and the "receiver" are usually not willing to offer information about the transaction to the police. Vital documentary evidence has to be gathered very quickly to prevent destruction.

As can be seen from the provisions of Section 5, the Act is now out of date and needs a thorough overhaul. The maximum ceiling for a fine under this Act is UShs. 20,000 and UShs. 40,000. Whereas this was a lot of money in 1970, our currency has lost its strength over the years such that these fines must be revised upwards to reflect today's value.

Elsewhere, we now also have the Leadership Code (Statute No. 8 of 1992). The Statute was passed to ensure minimum standards of behaviour. The Committee, however, is not yet functional, otherwise it would be an additional tool in the fight against corruption. In Ugandan law enforcement domain experience has shown that the mere passage of a law does not guarantee its implementation. The investigation of corruption requires sophistication because it usually involves a network of complex transactions (such as customs transactions, award of tenders, administration of estates, and so on). The Uganda police needs skilled police officers to make sense out of a particular transaction. This can be time consuming and requires the aid of other disciplines. It requires a well-honed understanding of law since there is always a tendency towards a wide interpretation of what constitutes the offence of corruption, an administrative violation or what is in fact not violation at all. Currently, we are trying to improve on the syllabus of the police training institutions in the country, because we discovered that police education was poorly equipped to address the unique aspects created by not only the Prevention of Corruption Act itself, but also all the other laws relating to fraud generally. We are also still lacking in the integration of investigators, skilled and trained, who are equally adept at prosecuting such cases. These are not only serious problems that must be resolved–they represent another critical element essential to the investigation of cases of corruption and fraud.

Most of the cases of corruption operate on the fringes of legality and illegality. The distinctions are usually blurred and difficult to discern. There is always a problem, for example, of distinguishing a genuine gift and corruption.

The fight against corruption is long and dreary. It is therefore necessary that opportunities for corruption are plugged through systematic and frequent review of administrative policies, improvement in procedures and instructions. Leadership and supervisory control must also be strengthened. While the total elimination of corruption from a system may be utopian, one cannot ignore the fact that corruption prevention techniques, if adopted consciously and rationally by the management, would go a long way in cleansing business organisations and government departments.

Part Six

ROLE OF THE MEDIA

14 The state of the media in Uganda

Amos Kajoba

Uganda is right now going through a historical process in which the press has a powerful and vital role to play.

An assessment of the state of the media must of necessity produce differences in opinion, not only among "observers" but also among the journalists themselves. If this happens, then it is healthy and it ought to be the case if we acknowledge from the outset that there are varying, sometimes opposing, perceptions of what role the media must play in society. There is never going to be a universal consensus.

What is important is to uphold the principle of pluralism in all spheres of public life and to ensure that mass media pluralism is defended and protected at all costs, against any tendency towards any form of monopoly of mass communication. In particular, we must guard against any tendency to shut out views that are different from the views of those in authority or those who own and a control mass media.

Background

One cannot effectively assess the media today without looking at the historical foundations of the media. Uganda's press has had a rather checkered history from its beginning in 1897 when the British colonial administration set up the *Royal Gazette*, the forerunner of the state-owned media. This was followed by the *Mengo Notes* of the Church Missionary Society in 1900.

The history of the press in Uganda has since reflected political shifts in the country. Before independence, there was a vibrant press in the country. The advent of independence, the 1966-67 crises, the declaration of a state of emergency in Buganda from 1966-71 and 1969-71, in the rest of the country, and above all, Amin's regime all contributed to the demise of the press.

In 1979, there was a relaxation of state restrictions on the press. This was however short-lived. It was again curtailed in 1981. This was not helped by the bush war that was ravaging parts of the country. During this time, the mainstream media only reflected the "official" position.

How did this state monopoly curtail press freedom? All governments, post-colonial governments in Uganda including that of NRM, have at certain stages tried to use the press to advance their interests. In order to use somebody, you must control him. Governments have tried to control the media using British-derived laws. These have since then been modified to fit the whims of those in authority at any one time.

The Press Censorship Act, which forms the basis of press censorship in Uganda, came into force in 1972. It was amended again to become decree No. 35. This gave the ministers discretion to ban any paper. It was invoked in 1974 and 1975 to ban the sale of and distribution of all 'imperialist' papers in Uganda. In 1980 three papers were banned. Furthermore, less than three months, after the 1980 elections, government banned four newspapers.

These laws have always been invoked by different governments to terminate or suspend press freedom.

The press has always been under intense political pressure. Governments have always viewed non conformity in reporting as subversive. The press has always been accused of assuming the role of some sort of unofficial opposition.

At times, press freedom has been curtailed by pressmen who want to gain favour by becoming sycophants. In 1970, the then Editor of *The People* newspaper was calling for total control of the press and nationalisation of all foreign-owned media. Even today, there are some journalists who want papers like *The People* proscribed.

Governments have also invoked laws which do not directly affect the media to "tame" journalists, like deporting foreign journalists from *Time* magazine in 1965 for violating the Secrets Act. Their presence in the country was not considered conducive to order and stability. In 1973 Philip Short of Reuters was deported for filing allegedly damaging reports.

There have been various attempts to "tame" Ugandan journalists with detention, dubious arrests as well as veiled and overt threats. Governments have also persecuted journalists through torture, harassment and banning of papers. The arrest and detention of Bob Kitimbo and Jimmy Luyima led to the closure of *Munno* in 1976.

Government policies, particularly on the economic front, may have been contributory to the state of the media. The economic policies pushed up the cost of production, reduced the literacy level, drastically reduced the purchasing power of the majority of potential readers, thus limiting the market expansion, improvement of quality, quantity and distribution of the newspapers and reduced the ability to recruit well trained staff and to motivate them adequately. This has been compounded by discriminatory allocation of advertisements and subscriptions in the private media.

There have also been attempts to frustrate the local media by giving red carpet treatment to foreign journalists who are exempted from persecutions and repression. They have been used to cleanse government's dark activities and to misrepresent real and imagined enemies.

Well, this is changing. Informal meetings with President Museveni and his ministers is an indicator that the attitude towards the local media is changing.

NRM Era

The ten-year NRM rule has been the longest period during which the press has enjoyed some freedom.

It is during this time that we have witnessed the birth of a number of papers representing varied political and social groups and an equal number of publication deaths, some after a few sporadic issues.

Today, there are about 35 publications out of which seven are state-owned and the others private or para-private. Of these, three are dailies, one tri-weekly, four bi-weekly, 13 weekly, eight-monthly and two-quarterly. Twenty-one are in English, while the rest are in local languages.

It is during this period that the mass communication programme was born at Makerere University, various training programmes were introduced locally and increased overseas opportunities offered to journalists.

The press now has better educated, more professionally trained and better exposed personnel. This has certainly brought improvements in almost all aspects, in content and form.

It is obvious from the above, that 1986 opened the gates for the media. This was due to several factors which include global developments, particularly the end of the cold war.

The NRM leaders rode to power on the back of propaganda in the media. They therefore appreciated the role and power of the press in their struggle for power and the maintenance of that power once acquired.

Consequently, the NRM recruited high-powered and skilled communicators in its team mainly for propaganda dissemination and for disinformation so as to hide the NRM's real goals of acquiring political power, the covering up of atrocities and the establishment of a one-party state.

As a result, a number of papers sprung up with literally no restriction in their path. Many journalists and non journalists alike set up papers. At one time, we had as many as 40 publications on the streets although their mortality rate was as high as their birth rate.

The rise and fall of newspapers and magazines bothers me occasionally for the simple reason that it gives certain signals for instability in a profession which has a vital and powerful role to play in moving forward. Otherwise how does one explain the collapse of *Munno* and *Topic* at a time when the media has had the longest uninterrupted period of press freedom?

Of course the publication and marketing of newspapers are conditioned by the laws of supply and demand.

With so many papers on the media landscape, it did not take long for some papers to show negative trends like sensationalism and disregard of the professional ethics. This led to public criticism and a call for control and guidance, and discipline of the media.

Leading the attack were the government officials, including key personalities like President Museveni, his ministers and some members of the public.

The press was accused of sensationalism and the publication of half truths. Its commitment to national security became questionable. These "excesses" were invariably regarded by the critics as attempts to destabilise the country through "irresponsible" journalism.

Most of the attacks were politically motivated, since such criticism did not recognise the vital role that the press was playing in exposing abuse of office, corruption and serving as a restraining factor on excesses of government. Of course, some of our colleagues went beyond the limits, violating ethics, over-personalising issues and the relative freedom we enjoy has gone into our heads, making a section of the press socially irresponsible.

Every cloud has a silver lining. This daredevil, irresponsible media however opened a new chapter for the media in the country. It pioneered investigative reporting and particularly of corruption by big politicians and government officials.

In its attempt to control the press the government indicated its intention to introduce the Mass Media Bill way back in 1987. This bill saw the coming and falling of four ministers of Information and Attorneys -General. It kept travelling between the Ministry of Information and Justice, Cabinet and the NRC. This was basically due to the fight put up by journalists against the oppressive bill.

In between the state continued to fight the media. In 1988, *The Weekend Digest* was banned. In 1992, four Editors were arrested, detained and charged. When the journalists complained about government's and especially the Army's increasing intolerance of serious criticism, Museveni retorted: "You may write as much as you want about me, but not about my army."

Immediately afterwards, he had a law enacted in the NRC prohibiting or proscribing the press from writing anything considered by the regime as defamatory to NRA. This law had a very scaring effect on the journalists, so much so that many inhumane acts by the NRA did and continue to pass unreported in the local press because journalists fear being victimised on the basis of the law.

Several editors and journalists have been arrested and charged. The cases of Festo Ebongu, Alfred Okware and Hussein Abdi, who were arrested for asking former President Kenneth Kaunda embarrassing questions, Lawrence Kiwanuka for sedition, and Henry Mirima who was arrested because Kiwanuka for whom he had stood surety had jumped bail are still fresh. The recent arrest of the Editors of the *Monitor, Shariat* and *Uganda Confidential* are all attempts at guiding, controlling and disciplining the press by government.

In 1995, government thought enough was enough and brought back the Media Bill. The bill consolidated a number of laws relating to publications and other modes of transmission of information while enhancing, emphasizing and consolidating its repressive aspects. Eventually the print media was separated from the electronic media.

There is a tendency to regard the press as a medium through which the government may reach the people rather than one through which the people may reach the government.

The journalists put up a spirited fight but in the end lost. The Print Media Bill was passed and it is now the Press and Journalists Statute 1995. The most important thing that was achieved is the recognition of journalism as a profession. Journalists are the majority on the Media Council and control the professional body - The National Institute of Journalists of Uganda (NIJU).

The statute however overlooked the fact that the majority of media personnel who have kept the media running did not meet the qualification set out in the statute and did not give them a grace period.

Although on the surface it looks like the media is in control, there is a lot of room for government to intervene. He who has the right and power to give has the right and power to withdraw.

Electronic media

In a country where the population is traditionally oral and the majority have no access to newspapers due to low purchasing power and illiteracy, electronic media, particularly radio, plays an important role as an instrument of enlightenment, education and entertainment.

Like in many other territories, broadcasting was introduced in Uganda by the colonialists as a service to the settler community, basically to provide them with news, reaffirm their authority and to sustain cultural links with their imperial centre.

Radio Uganda started in 1952/53 and went on air in 1954 with short messages, news and announcements in English and Luganda. Since then, Radio Uganda has expanded to cater for almost all Ugandan languages. Today, the station broadcasts in 22 local languages and two national languages: English and Kiswahili.

Radio Uganda has remained a government mouthpiece, with little or no news to stimulate development. Radio control is exercised through censorship which makes news boring such that people tend to depend on foreign news to know about certain sensitive matters in Uganda.

Censorship was more pronounced during Amin's regime when everything had to be cleared by the Permanent Secretary (PS). This resulted in the transfer of the Radio newsroom and news studio from broadcasting house to Nakasero where the PS was based. However, with the coming of the National Resistance Movement, the newsroom was taken back to its former place.

Broadcasting has also been liberalised. Private individuals and institutions have been allowed to start private stations. So far several private FM stations are fully operational and many more are in the pipeline.

These new commercial radio stations have concentrated on entertainment at the expense of education and enlightenment of society.

The idea of television was first put forward by the British Colonial Secretary in 1957 in an attempt to promote British companies, British culture and assist smooth colonial administration. However, this was shelved in preference for improvement of broadcasting.

The hope for television was revived at independence and in 1963 a cabinet paper on TV indicating its benefits was tabled. Uganda Television was then inaugurated on October 8, 1963.

News bulletins are the item important on UTV as reflected by the time allocated even as far back as 1965. Today UTV broadcasts news everyday in three languages: Luganda, Swahili and English for between 20-30 minutes each.

Until 1982, both Radio Uganda and UTV news bulletins were edited in one newsroom. When UTV went video in 1980 it became necessary for it to edit its own news. However, complete separation came in 1991. Today UTV has its own reporters and news editors though it still relies heavily on Uganda News Agency that also feeds Radio Uganda with news.

Like broadcasting, television airwaves have been liberalised and private individuals and institutions have been allowed to set up TV stations. Right now there are three private television stations operating but like radio they basically concentrate on entertainment.

Radio Uganda and Uganda Television are government mouthpieces. Although there is no direct government editorial policy on the news contents, directives to guide the news are often sent by the Permanent Secretary, Ministry of Information, to the editors.

In practical terms, press freedom boils down to insulating the media from government control, interference, undue influence and intimidation. UJA is a voluntary, non statutory and independent "professional" body. Its existence is not affected in any way by statutory organs. If organised with clear objectives and a clear programme, UJA would mirror the level and strength of press freedom in Uganda. The onus is on the journalists to organise themselves and to shed government control, interference and influence.

Most of the journalists in this country take issues that affect them for granted. At the time of debating the Electronic Media Bill by Parliament, none of the media people, not even those involved in the electronic media, said a word, yet it contains many unfavourable articles. It was passed in that form. It is now law. The press is yet to learn to educate and mobilise the public to understand and appreciate the cause of a free press, that freedom of expression, speech and the press is freedom for all.

The greatest challenge facing the press is that of building the foundations upon which future freedoms will thrive. This is where UJA and other journalists' bodies have a very big role to play.

Journalists made submissions to the Constitutional Commission calling for the entrenchment of freedom of the press and the guarantee of access to information.

Article 29 of the 1995 constitution guarantees freedom of speech and expression, which includes freedom of the press. Article 41 guarantees every citizen access to information in the possession of the state or any other organ or agency.

The new constitution has certainly opened new frontiers for the practice of journalism in Uganda. Our past and very recent history has thrown up new challenges and responsibilities for all professionals. As one of the recognised pillars of democratic rule, our responsibilities and challenges have assumed greater complexities and dimensions. From a suffocating and destructive culture of silence we have made a transition to a culture of expression.

The once unipolar media landscape dotted with only "the state-owned government controlled Press" has changed into a refreshing one in which a thousand ideas and a million flowers have blossomed and flourished. Instead of monologues and one-way pontifications by an oligarcy, we now have debate and dialogue. It can be argued that not every voice is being heard, but we take strength and comfort from the knowledge that, unlike in the past when we all sang one song, different songs can be heard today. This is good for governance and democracy. It purifies and strengthens the social contract under which citizens are governed or misgoverned.

It is now up to the journalists to seize the freedom the constitution has given us and to make the press a vital institution for protection and promotion of democracy.

But for the press to be part of the salvation and not part of the problem, for the press to positively influence events, for us to strengthen and internalise democracy in this country, we need to constantly and continually assess ourselves and ask ourselves with the help of those who watch, listen and read us whether we are fulfilling our pledge to be faithful and true soldiers for progress, whether we are quick to assert that the press is the watchdog over the people's interests vis-a-vis the performance of those who govern, whether we are moulders or not of opinion in society. If we claim we are the measuring rod for freedom of expression in society, then we need also to seriously be aware of the high demands society imposes on us. We can only be aware through constantly reviewing our performance in fora like this one.

Reporting/writing skills

Political issues still dominate our papers at the expense of developmental, educational and environmental news. The media is strong in exposing official malpractice, but still weak in analysing and exposing shortcomings in policies. Our media is weakest in handling economic matters. Most of the stories on the economy are propaganda or public relations stories.

Editing and packing

The art of editing a text and improving copy is still weak, there is a waste of space using 20 words for one, a full page for a story that would take a quarter of a page. There is more preaching than provision of information. Politicians still take up a large proportion of space in papers. Some papers still suffer from poor layout and design, printing at times is awful, picture production is at times disappointing as is production and circulation. Lastly, the media is still urban based and elitist.

Cost

The high cost of production threatens the sustenance of press pluralism. Something needs to be done about taxes, because when access to media is very expensive, the people's right to information and participation in public affairs is impaired. We all know that tyranny survives on ignorance and ignorance nourishes underdevelopment.

Low capitalisation of media enterprises has had a negative impact on standards of journalism. We cannot run away from the fact that high standards of the media depend on its capability to attract highly qualified and experienced personnel, and their ability to invest money in the process of gathering information requires resources.

Management

Another problem facing the media industry is lack of media management skills by owners and editors of most newspapers. The management of newspapers is quite different from management of other business concerns. Most business people enter the industry without taking this into consideration.

Secondly, until recently most journalism training institutions did not include management and accounts on their syllabi. As a result, most good editors have been poor managers of personnel and resources, leading to the collapse of newspapers.

Circulation

Uganda newspaper circulation, though it appears to be at its highest, still falls short of the UNESCO-recommended goal of 100 copies for 1000 people. Quite a large proportion of the people, particularly in rural areas, do not come in touch with a newspaper.

Most of the problems enumerated here could be minimised with increased capitalisation for the independent press. The problem of cash flow affects the breadth and depth of coverage. Some of the journalists and media proprietors have often times had occasion to review their performance but such reviews need to be done more rigorously to ensure the maintenance and improvement of media professionalism and service delivery. Today's forum provides a platform for a much broader review and cross fertilisation of divergent views on the press, and its role should be encouraged so that the media becomes one of the pillars of the new constitutional order and good governance in Uganda.

Conclusion

The media landscape in this country, as elsewhere, has been a subject of varied comments. There has been heated and emotional debate on the performance of the press. The focus on the press reflects a recognition of the power of the media to either retard or advance the development and progress of an individual, firm, community or nation.

In playing its watchdog role, the question has at times been asked about who watches over the watchdog in his role of entertaining, informing and educating the whole spectrum of society.

Journalists, as professionals, operate within a wide environment in which other actors come into play. It is therefore important for journalists to receive the support and appreciation of the wider society as well as its critical views and comments. The media in Uganda should play its role, among other plays, in the development of a viable, accountable, transparent and democratic culture in Uganda.

15 The Media: A Pillar in Fighting Corruption

Eric Ogoso Opolot

Introduction

Dubbed the 4th estate, the media is one of the strongest pillars of civil society. It plays a very significant role in fighting corruption. But journalists, like any other professionals, need to be prepared, trained, and facilitated to be effective in their work.

In Uganda, there are about 400 journalists working in the print, electronic and broadcast media. About 40 publications including 5 dailies, one tri-weekly, 4 bi-weeklies, 13 weeklies and 81 monthlies exist currently. There are also 5 private radio stations and 3 private TV stations operating alongside the government TV and radio.

Under the NRM government, the waves have been liberalised and more media organisations may come up.

The ten years of NRM rule have been the most prosperous for the Ugandan media. But, as is the case with new changes, the media itself is overwhelmed by the freedom it enjoys and the opportunities for growth that are available. In some instances, this has manifested itself as failure to comprehend the limits and limitations of that freedom while in other cases it has manifested itself as outright abuse.

Nevertheless, the benefits from press freedom have enabled the existence and growth of a vibrant, aggressive and largely responsible media. Publications in Uganda today range from more moderate papers to extremely radical papers. *Uganda Confidential* - the paper that advertises itself as one that splits the atom – is one such publication. In its extremely radical writing, the paper though has proved a leading crusader against corruption.

The Monitor has also on many an occasion published well researched stories exposing graft, while *The New Vision* as well as *The Crusader* are getting increasingly aggressive in exposing corruption.

The case of *The New Vision* is unique. The paper is owned by the government but on several occasions it has exposed graft within the same government. For a government-owned publication to criticise its owner without getting compromised is an interesting development in press freedom in Uganda.

Both within the country and outside it, the Ugandan media is gaining increasing respect. Several stories in the media have been a subject of debate in parliament. Others have caused action to be taken. *The New Vision*, for instance, broke a story about an 84-million dollar project to build a dam at Jinja in 1996.

The Chinese firm which won the contract for the project did a substandard job. The Chinese would have got away with it if the paper had not broken the story. The first story saying the Chinese were doing a shoddy job drew a lot of wrath from various quarters including some people in government who thought the paper simply wanted to spoil the good relations between China and Uganda. A lot of people were angered.

Then the paper ran another story and yet another. Again people were upset. A few more stories and the Chinese lost the contract. A commission of enquiry was eventually set up by the government to probe allegations that the Chinese spent 30% of the 84 million dollars to bribe Ugandan officials to get the tender award. At the time of writing, fresh bids have been invited for the project. And the Uganda government is considering taking the Chinese to court.

Another story that had an impact involved a group of Kenyan students who were fraudulently admitted into Makerere university. The 91 students came to Uganda but their admissions were fake and they could not be taken into the university. Yet they had paid a lot of money to a bogus NGO that arranged their 'admission' into Makerere. The papers exposed the matter and eventually the Kenyans were taken back home by their government.

They lost their money and the opportunity to study at the university. There have been other exposes that have had significant impact. A story on a medical professor that fleeced AIDS patients of millions of shillings by claiming to cure the disease led to his drugs being banned by the Uganda government.

Another story about smuggling of chimps out of Uganda drew public attention to the plight of chimps – one of the world's endangered animals – and action was taken to close one of the most lucrative illegal lines of business in Uganda. There was also a story about a cement factory that spewed tons of dust into the atmosphere just because the owners did not want to meet the cost of installing filters.

After several stories in the papers, the owners eventually installed the expensive filter. Today the factory has stopped spewing dust into the neighbouring villages.

The need to train

But to be effective, investigative journalists need to be trained, facilitated and equipped to do their job. Investigative journalism, like any other serious business, does not come cheap.

When the Economic Development Institute (EDI) and the Inspectorate of Government in Uganda recognised the need to train the members of this pillar of civil society in 1995, and decided to organise a series of investigative journalism workshops, it was the opportunity every journalist needed.

The workshops were one of the outcomes of the recommendations of a December 1994 conference sponsored by Transparency International, the EDI of the World Bank, and the Inspectorate of Government in Uganda. That conference concluded with a proposed Action Plan to assist the Uganda government to fight corruption, hence one that needed training.

The overall objectives of the workshops were to develop the capacity of Ugandan journalists to investigate and publish researched stories, especially those targeted at exposing corruption, and to strengthen journalism in the region through development of a network that could enhance journalistic output.

At the end of each of the workshops, it was thought that the journalists would take a more active, constructive part in the implementation of democratisation; be better informed, more aware and more assertive of their rights.

It was also thought that the journalists would help ensure higher standards of clean, accountable and transparent government; and be able to reject corruption as anti-social behaviour.

All the workshops included a simulated case study called "Freedonia" – breaking a story in a fictitious country called Freedonia and mainly in its capital Aquanaba.

The simulated study highlighted corruption and lack of transparency in the workings of a government and implied possible corrupt practices involved in land disposal and in the building of a luxury development scheme in place of a squatter settlement. It proved the most popular aspect of the course.

The investigative journalism workshops

Six such workshops have since been held including two exclusively for women journalists. The response and interest in them has been overwhelming.

During the 3rd and 4th workshops which were exclusively for women at Colline Hotel Mukono, the participants signed a pledge called the Mukono Commitment, which reads thus:

1. We shall in all respects uphold and advance the highest standards of the profession of journalism.
2. We will in our personal conduct, and in our dealings with others, act in a responsible and dedicated fashion, and will reject and condemn the conduct of others when it offends journalistic ethics and/or is corrupt.
3. Recognising that corruption is damaging our country's development, we will in our work expose corruption wherever we can unearth it, we shall ensure that the public is made aware of the damage being caused to everyone by the grand corruption of a comparative few and help build a public climate of opinion which rejects corrupt conduct.

This particular workshop was addressed by Mr de Speville, head of the anti-corruption commission in Hong Kong who shared his experience with the participants both in a formal session and at a cocktail.

This idea of a pledge was later borrowed at the first investigative journalism workshop for Tanzania in Arusha in May 1996. Two Ugandans including myself were honoured to facilitate at that workshop and we kick-started a process of investigative journalism training which has to date caught on in Tanzania.

The Arusha pledge was more detailed and more committing than the Ugandan one but we saw it all as part of an irreversible struggle. Arusha is East Africa's capital and so we felt it was the right place to make the pledge to fight corruption

One unique aspect of that workshop was a discussion of corruption in the Tanzanian media which emanated almost spontaneously. It was a heated discussion in which participants criticised each other frankly. Next day it was the lead story in the Tanzania newspapers. 'How clean is the Tanzanian media?' read one headline.

Interestingly, a report of the Presidential Commission Against Corruption issued 10 months later implicated the journalists themselves in corruption. The secretary to the commission, Mr Alex Muganda, was at the Arusha workshop but never at any one point mentioned that he was investigating the journalists as well.

Methodology

A strong point of the investigative journalism training programme in Uganda is the approach used. The pedagogical framework in the workshop was the division of the participants into groups – four groups working on the Freedonial Case Study, and four others working on the field trip.

Through group work interspersed with plenary sessions the participants were exposed to sets of theoretical, semi-practical and practical activities. Lectures were also presented as part of the workshop.

Basically, the workshop used a hands-on approach, a real life approach, simulation and a confidence-building approach.

The hands-on approach was highly participatory. The journalists were actively engaged in practical exercises, discussions, plenary discussions of personal experiences, and a mix of all these scenarios. Throughout the workshops, the participants wrote articles, lead stories, and plans of action. The stories were analysed by the participants themselves in plenary sessions. Participants were free to send their stories to their newspapers for publication.

The real-life approach aimed to ensure that the workshop remained relevant to the participants' daily lives. It made clear to the participants that they themselves were the experts while the instructors were merely facilitators. Throughout the workshop, the participants were encouraged to share their personal experiences. A full day of field investigation was set aside for them to experience real-life situations in the field.

The simulation using 'Freedonia' was a major skill-building component of the workshop whose essence was to encourage the participants to dip under the surface of ordinary news stories, to find 'the nose of the hippo', to find 'the iceberg below the ice-tip'.

The simulation was a continually unfolding story with four journals to which the participants were free to belong, competing to carry the best story. Each day in the exercise, the newsrooms would receive new information, decide what to do with it and write stories.

The exercise had several traps and pitfalls along the way and participants had to exercise a lot of skill, judgement and experience in developing story lines. Perhaps it suffices to say at this point that the Freedonia experience has now been put on the internet by EDI as a self-training simulation exercise. This is a major outcome of our training activities.

In building confidence, the intention was to foster an atmosphere of absolute trust between resource persons, participants, organisers and anybody who was involved in the workshop. It was felt this was the best way to ensure that issues were discussed by all freely and without fear or favour.

The feedback from these workshops showed a close and productive relationship between the classroom exercises and real-life experiences.

An advanced investigative journalism workshop has since been held which was attended by those who had attended the previous workshops. Among other activities, a commitment to fight corruption was renewed by participants.

Conclusion

Interest in these workshops is clearly growing. In the 6th basic workshop held in March 1997, at the Uganda Management Institute, Kampala, six participants more than those invited turned up. They offered to pay for their own costs at the course including feeding and accommodation.

This particular workshop was planned, organised and facilitated entirely by Ugandans. For the first time we did not involve foreign facilitators in the workshop - except for former Tanzanian Prime Minister Joseph Warioba, the Tanzanian Anti-Corruption Commission Secretary Alex Muganda, Transparency International's Jeremy Pope and EDI's Petter Langseth and Rich Stapenhurst. But even these were limited to only paper presentations.

As had happened before, that workshop was generously supported by DANIDA and the Uganda Management Institute.

Though a detailed, evaluation of these workshops is yet to be conducted, a glance at the performance of the 200 or so journalists who attended these workshops shows an improvement in levels of investigation. The improvement is small but noticeable. There are more stories highlighting corruption in the media these days than ever before. There is no doubt that the training programme has had a positive impact. So which way the future?

We cannot run away from the struggle against corruption now. At times it looks a futile struggle but there are indicators that some gains are being made. To this end, more training is necessary, now and for years to come. But future training programmes should be designed to suit a wide range of journalists with varying skills and experiences. Sources of local funding also need to be identified so as to ensure sustainability of the training programmes. As the late Kwame Nkrumah said 'backwards never, forward ever.'

Lastly, it might interest the readers to take a look at the detailed content of one of our workshops held for women at Mukono and one of the products the journalists at the workshops produced. The product was a daily 'newspaper' for our participants produced by themselves using a laptop computer, a printer and a photocopier.

16 Investigative Journalism: The Mutual Roles of the Media and the Civil Service in Exposing Misconduct

James Katorobo

What is investigative journalism?

Journalism may be defined as the collection and processing of facts about current events for dissemination to the public through the medium of newspapers, magazines, radio, television, and so on. In most cases minimal research may be necessary to get the information. In easier cases, those who have the information are willing to make it easily available to the journalists. The cases of concern in this paper are when the information is hidden or covered up. These cases call for sustained investigation. Considerable effort may be required to unearth the hidden facts. These facts may be embarrassing if disclosed. In more serious cases, the facts may lead to political liability. As a result, those likely to be adversely affected by the disclosures may take protective or defensive measures to prevent access to the information or publication of the information if already acquired. Investigative journalism is therefore the collection, processing, and publication of information about important events and occurrences that call for considerable investigative effort, skills, and commitment.

The needs and limits of investigative journalism in Uganda

The need for investigative journalism in Uganda is very high. However, the scope of investigative journalism by the major papers (*The New Vision*, *The Monitor*, *The Citizen*) is limited. Yet these are the papers with the potential to undertake investigative journalism. They have strength in terms of mass circulation, capacity to mobilise resources, and command of skilled journalists. There are several reasons why their performance in investigative journalism is limited.

The New Vision is a government paper and as such it is inhibited from exposing official misconduct that would tarnish the government. While *The Monitor* can be considered on anti-government paper, it can sustain a critical portrayal of government activities based on stories, accounts, and news items that are readily available and that do not demand considerable investigative effort. It carries a few such stories and then the bulk of the paper is filled with sensational reports and jokes, most of it sexist. Thus the large mass circulation papers have adequate, readily available reports and do not have to invest a considerable effort in original data gathering about possible hidden misdeeds.

There is another group of papers that can be deemed anti-government (*The Shariat* is the best example) that depend on taking limited facts and building (creating) anti-government stories out of them. These papers are dominated by malice and engage in partial and inadequate investigative journalism. Their main purpose is to condemn and undermine, not necessarily to reveal the truth, inform, and educate. Another example is *The Exposure*. Judging by its title it should be a paper based largely on investigative journalism; but the paper is so strongly anti-government that its investigative contributions are largely negative. In *The Exposure* (March 1995, No. 64) the Editor-in-Chief, Henry F. Mirima, is shown riding a bicycle to cover the Buseruka rebel attack on the Buseruka Police Post. This conforms to the criterion of effort that is characteristic of investigative journalism. However, investigative journalism on rebel activities has discredited itself in two ways.

First, the reporting was malicious and betrayed sympathy, or even support, for the rebel activities. Consider the following five titles in *The Exposure*:

- "It's Mpiso's Army Hitting" (*The Exposure*, March 1995)
- "Rebels' Case Presented in Europe" (*The Exposure*, April 1995)
- "Disarm NRA" (*The Exposure*, April 1995)
- "Veterans to be Dumped in Bunyoro, but Banyoro say NO" (*The Exposure*, April 1995)
- "Major Mpiso Attacking Police Stations in a Bid to Disarm All Security Personnel" (*The Exposure*, March 1995)

Clearly, choice of blatantly biased titles against the government cannot enhance the growth, development, and recognition of investigative journalism.

Second, a rebel group invited a journalist, the former editor of *The Citizen*, Mr. Lawrence Kiwanuka, to visit their rebel camp. He agreed and was taken blindfolded. He conducted an interview with the rebel leader, Major Herbert Itongwa. Kiwanuka's article was published by *The Citizen* and was a major scoop. *The Citizen*, 23 March 1995, that carried the article sold 10,000 copies, a three fold jump from its normal 3,000 weekly sales. *The New Vision* of March 24 that reprinted the article sold out 35,000 by midday. Judged from the point of view of significance and interest it was a major publication. But still this is not a good example of investigative journalism. There was no effort on the part of the journalist to investigate the rebel activities independently. The rebels needed a publication outlet and Kiwanuka was made the channel for that publicity. It also raised the possibility that the journalist was an accomplice in promoting rebel activities.

The media exposure of misconduct

Naked journalism may be defined as the presentation of reality as it is, without critical interpretation and analysis. For example, Swazi newspapers tend to present accounts of sex encounters as would be depicted in a movie. The raw facts are presented in raw language. This may be called innocent naked journalism. Reports and exposes in the *Uganda Confidential* are the presentation of official and sometimes private misconduct in raw language. These exposes are described in malicious graphical detail and made available to the *Uganda Confidential* by the protagonists. The editor of the *Uganda Confidential* dishes them out with minimal editorial processing for sensational public consumption. It conforms to the adage that facts speak for themselves. The editor has a tendency of focusing on particular public figures (Dr. Ruhakana Rugunda, Sir Rich Kaijuka, Tumusiime Mutebile). This never-ending focus on particular individuals gives the impression of a journalistic witch-hunt.

And so the motive behind's approach defies characterisation. Is it a journalistic moral crusade against corrupt officials? Is it journalistic malice against a regime that failed to reward 's self-proclaimed contribution to the NRM struggle? Is it pecuniary survival to promote sales and make money?

The *Confidential* fails to meet the standard of investigative journalism. The standard to be met is a dispassionate investment of energy into discovering and exposing hidden misconduct, not with malicious intent, but with the objective of promoting the public good. The *Confidential* moved in this direction, but remained at the level of malicious naked journalism.

The media promotion of investigative journalism

It should be the role of the media institutions to:

- promote a well informed public;
- enhance democracy and good governance;
- keep the public well informed about the activities of politicians (good or bad);
- keep the public well informed about the activities of civil servants (good or bad);
- make enough money to continue in the news dissemination business.

In achieving the above roles and objectives media institutions have to make a strategic choice between (i) undertaking minimal investigative journalism (*New Vision, Monitor, Citizen*) and (ii) undertaking mostly investigative journalism (*Confidential, , The Shariat, Exposure, Private Eye* in Britain).

Civil servants and promotion of investigative journalism

The role of civil servants is to ensure effective, efficient and equitable delivery of government services to the public. Civil servants derive recognition and esteem from media reports about their good performance. They also fear the consequences of adverse reports in the newspapers. Civil servants get in trouble with politicians if negative reports about poor performance appear in the news media. Public support for a government can decline to the point where the government is voted out of power. Media reports about civil service performance can make or unmake the government. As a result, the role played by civil servants in encouraging or discouraging investigative journalism depends on a careful analysis of the motives and objectives of different strategic types of civil servants.

Attitudes toward investigative journalism

The most important factor to take into account is the degree of the civil servants' involvement in the misconduct being investigated. Those civil servants involved in the misconduct will actively create difficulties for investigative journalism. A few of the civil servants not involved in the misconduct will actively assist investigative journalism. It should be realised that a majority of civil servants, even if not involved in the misconduct, will be indifferent. These provide opportunities for transforming latent support to active support. Others will be fearful of getting involved in investigative journalism.

Access to information and the importance of rank position

Excellent investigative journalism depends on access to concrete information on various issues of public interest or concern. The willingness of the civil servants to make it available to the investigative journalist depends on (i) the rank of the civil servants with higher civil servants having high access and lower civil servants low access, (ii) the type of civil servants' attitudes (allies, enemies, indifferent, or fearful), and (iii) a special category of information specialists, the information gatekeeper. The roles they may play in facilitating or frustrating investigative journalism is explored in Table 1 (below). High-ranking allies provide the best source of concrete evidence but they have to work within the limits of the Secrets Act. High-ranking enemies cause the greatest frustration.

Table 1: Type of Civil Servants and Access to Investigative Information

Types of Support of Civil Servants	High Rank Civil Servants	Low Rank Civil Servants
Allies of investigative journalism	These have the concrete documentary evidence but they may be restrained by the Secrets Act.	These are usually a source of gossip or rumours that can provide a starting point. But concrete documentary evidence is required.
Enemies of investigative journalism	These will actively hide the documentary evidence and if necessary destroy it.	These usually do the donkey work and get the hyena's share. These can provide the most reliable leads to the secrets.
The indifferent or fearful	The indifferent can be a source if persuaded. The fearful are to be avoided.	The indifferent can be a source if persuaded. The fearful are to be avoided.
Information gatekeepers (secretaries, computer operators, among others)	In these are allies they will release the information, if they are enemies, they will hide it.	If these are allies they will release the information, if they are enemies, they will hide it.

Human Rights and the promotion of the public good through the media

The potential conflict between protection of individual rights and promotion of the public good through investigative reporting can be illustrated by the confrontation between Patrick Kiggundu, a columnist for *The New Vision*, and the Hon. Katenta Apuuli, then Uganda's Ambassador to the United States a few years ago. In the article "Uganda's Sleeping Missions Abroad," The *Sunday Vision* of July 16, 1995 (pages 3 and 21), Patrick Kiggundu presented an analysis that is typical of investigative journalism. Mr. Kiggundu conducted investigations at Ugandan embassies abroad and demonstrated how ineffective they were. The main thrust of his argument was that most of the embassy staff devoted most of their time to the promotion of personal interests. The only ambassadors to be spared these criticisms were Prof. George Kirya in Britain and Dr. Tibamanya Mwene Mushanga in Canada.

Mr. Kiggundu did not pile up naked facts to speak for themselves. On the contrary, there were a balance between facts and interpretative social criticism. This is what made the article biting. Its conclusions were of profound public interest and the analysis had the potential of improving the public good.

But the Hon. Ambassador Katenta Apuuli wrote a scathing attack on Mr. Kiggundu's article regarding the performance of Uganda's embassy in Washington and of the behaviour of the ambassador himself. Ambassador Katenta Apuuli accused Mr. Kiggundu of misinformation and publication of falsehood. Katenta Apuuli even threatened to take the case to court unless Mr. Kiggundu retracted those comments and observations. The issue then was the human rights of Katenta Apuuli were greatly jeopardised in a report whose general consequences might be the enhancement of the public good of society?

In an attempt to defend himself, Katenta Apuuli ended by giving a detailed report of significant public interest on how the Uganda embassy in Washington had been managed. He also gave a very useful sketch of a model effective ambassador. Whatever the merits of the arguments of the two protagonists the significance in Patrick Kiggundu's work was that it was not particular embassies and particular ambassadors confined to but covered Uganda's missions in general. In contrast, the significance of Katenta Apuuli's self-defence was not his exoneration, but the explication of a standard of performance for all embassies.

This illustrates that individual rights may be violated in the promotion of the public good. What is important is to strike a balance such that the greatest public good is achieved through disclosure with minimal violation of individual rights. In the Katenta Apuuli case, his individual embarrassment must be seen against the public good that may have been derived from the investigative report.

Obstacles to investigative journalism

Our analysis of the scope and limits of investigative journalism in Uganda led us to the conclusion that while the opportunities abound for flourishing investigative journalism, there are significant obstacles that need to be overcome. Ten obstacles are identified and outlined seriatim below:

Journalism is costly

If there is enough information to fill up the pages of a daily such as *The New Vision* or *The Monitor,* why spend money on trying to search for hidden information? If readily available information is adequate, why incur expenses on costly research efforts?

Investigative journalism is highly risky

Penetrative, sustained investigation of misconduct (official or private) will induce defensive moves on the part of perpetrators to hide and cover up the information. They will try to destroy the information before it gets into the hands of the journalist. If the information is with the journalist, but not yet printed, they may try to steal it or even kill the journalist. If the information is already printed but not distributed, attempts may be made to stop distribution. In short, investigative journalism is extremely risky.

In the Lawrence Kiwanuka case he was on the horns of a dilemma. The information to which he was party was of interest to the government and to the rebels. It was like an individual fearing to move forward and be devoured by the lion or move backwards and be mauled by the tiger. If his report compromised either side, it guaranteed trouble. He was caught in what has been described as the double-bind jeopardy.

If investigative journalism is to flourish, there is a need to develop a code of conduct that will protect the parties involved. What is needed is a framework in which both government and rebels benefit from communicating with each other without harming the instrument (media) through whom the information is conveyed. Traditional kingdoms evolved a system of rules whereby messengers were not killed for conveying a negative message.

Inadequate commitment

It has already been pointed out that ordinary sources of information that do not require considerable investment of energy may be more than adequate to meet the raw materials that a newspaper needs. Thus, this line of least resistance is attractive to newspaper editors. They do not have to incur a lot of money in research and they are not likely to wake up ghosts hidden in government closets. This editorial policy ensures peace on all fronts. It means that most newspaper editors will not have the necessary commitment to meet the costs involved in investigative journalism.

What happens then is that those who have the commitment are usually motivated by malice. It may be an editor who wants to settle past scores with the government. This kind of motivation puts investigative journalism on a collision course with the government. It also causes the editor not to abide by the ethical codes and standards of objective and fair reporting.

The most acceptable and reliable basis of commitment is the devotion to unearthing the truth about the nature of the misconduct and to follow rational and scientific procedures in getting to that truth. What this means is that there is a great need to inculcate devotion to the truth as a standard of investigative journalism and to promote this belief through training and other forms of incentives.

Deficiencies in investigative skills

We have already remarked about the exposure of naked facts received from malicious sources intended to settle scores. It points to deficiencies in journalistic skills. Journalism is a profession with relevant skills that have to be learned and mastered. One of the critical problems of journalism in general is that many journalists have not been exposed to the body of knowledge and methods which they have to master in order to become effective on their job.

If investigative journalism is to flourish, then the following skill areas need to be mastered:

- Investigative research skills (obtrusive and non obtrusive).
- Analytical skills to translate raw data into effective stories and accounts.
- Writing information and persuasive articles (accounts) or exposes.
- Communication skills to get the information, to package it, and to disseminate it appropriately.

- A capacity to make sound social and political judgements.
- A capacity to balance journalistic courage, objectivity, and tact.
- A capacity for timeliness that avoids recklessness.

Independence or autonomy from government control

In the past most media institutions were controlled by the government. It was therefore impossible for editors to criticise the government which employed them. While pro-government media institutions remain dominant, the monopoly has been broken. A diversity of independent media have emerged. Government officials continue to favour government media institutions. It is therefore critical that non-government media define strategies for getting information from official sources and break the advantage that government media enjoy.

There is also a need to assist the government media to develop investigative journalism within the limits of their operation. Indeed investigative publications by the government-controlled media are much more likely to convince the government to act than publications seen to emanate from hostile sources.

Assisting anti-government journalists in becoming more analytical and impartial

The critique of anti-government papers is that they depend on dishing out raw data that is often distorted to cast government in a "bad light" and to increase circulation based on sensationalist reporting. Most of this reporting is deficient in terms of evidence of:

- Thorough and systematic collection of relevant facts and information.
- Analytical processing of the data to arrive at logical and consistent findings and conclusions.
- Statement of these facts without malice and distortion.
- Devotion to the absolute truth.

If anti-government or non-government media institutions could be trained to avoid the above errors, then the quality of their investigative journalism would improve and their credibility as a source of reliable and valid information would be enhanced. If their credibility could be enhanced, then senior government officials (those classified as allies) would be more willing to provide information knowing that it would be used properly to promote the public good.

The perceptions about the Secrets Act

The Secrets Act was not intended to protect information about misconduct. If government's intended actions were prematurely disclosed, this could lead to a breakdown of the capacity of government to act. It should be clear that forthcoming tax measures, or even worse, military movements, should never be disclosed.

This, however, does not mean that a civil servant should not disclose planned or ongoing corrupt activities. It stands to reason that the Secrets Act does not protect misconduct. Yet most officials believe that no government information shall be disclosed whatsoever. There is therefore a need to re-educate civil servants as to the boundaries of the Secrets Act and to enable them to disclose government misconduct in the public interest.

Freedom of Information Act

It should be realised that most governments in developing countries, while having the form of secrecy, are to a large extent exposed. Informal channels exist that ensure that a top secret is known before the ink is dry.

Many government files end up in markets as wrapping paper for goods traded in markets. The widespread use of government files as wrapping paper has been mitigated somewhat by the production of the environmentally hazardous 'kavera' (polythene paper). Yet loss of government records is still rampant. In any case officials have no time to actively make detailed records.

Thus we should be wary of believing that the government has massive data to which the citizen should have access as is the case in developed countries. However, it is worth while to pre-empt the emergence of this condition in the future by:

- Limiting information that may be classified as secret.
- Declassifying and reducing the time for which secrets may be kept.
- Putting in place a Freedom of Information Act to give citizens the right to access information kept by government about them.

Cultivating alliances within the Civil Service

One of the major obstacles to investigative journalism is the perception of generalised hostility by the civil service as a whole. This is erroneous.

Journalists need to be trained to strategically identify allies in the civil service who are willing to promote investigative journalism, to enlist their support and build a mutual relationship to achieve the common objective of an efficient, effective, and equitable civil service. It follows that they should also identify the enemies of investigative journalism in order to avoid them and at best neutralise their efforts to cover up information.

Building mutual confidence between civil servants and journalists

Reformist civil servants need to recognise and tap the opportunities created by investigative journalism. They should assist journalists to expose misconduct occurring in the civil service. They should also endeavour to actively overcome acts of cover-up by those engaged in misconduct. They should forge, enhance and promote mutual relations with investigative journalists to achieve the common objective of efficiency, effectiveness and equity.

Part Seven

INTERNATIONAL PARTNERS

17 Building Integrity to Fight Corruption: a Partnership Between Uganda, TI and EDI to Improve Service Delivery to the Public

Petter Langseth

The task of combating world-wide corruption is receiving support from the highest levels of the World Bank as evidenced by its inclusion in the President's Strategic Compact. It is now one of the issues that inform the formation of the Bank's lending activities. As the Bank finds itself with more information and more experience, which can be transferred to others, the challenge is to integrate anti-corruption work within the Bank without its financial dynamism and overall direction of the world economy.

The rationale for combating and containing corruption is not because corruption is "immoral", "wrong", or even illegal. Rather, it is because of the negative impact of corruption on economic development and on the emergence of an enabling environment for the private sector, and its role in deepening poverty in the developing world. Levels of corruption are revealed most starkly in the provision - or lack of it - of quality services to the public, and in the existence of a civil service more interested in serving itself, than in serving the public.

The involvement of the Bank in dealing with corruption per se is of comparatively recent origin. Whilst parts of the Bank have worked on some of the relevant areas - such as the judiciary and the rule of law - this has been in the context of the enforcement of contracts rather than in containing corruption as such.

This ground-breaking work commenced in Uganda and Tanzania and was conducted by EDI in collaboration with the anti-corruption non-governmental organisation, Transparency International (TI). Like EDI, TI did not claim to know the answers to the challenge but shared EDI's belief that answers would vary from society to society, and that solutions imposed from outside were not likely to succeed. TI also believed that in the past governments' efforts had failed where these did not enjoy the confidence and support of civil society, and that it was thus essential to develop broad coalitions in support of reform. An indifferent and disbelieving public could compromise even the best intentions of a government.

At the core of this approach lies the conviction that any programme of reform must be wholly owned and driven by internal actors, but that in the fashioning of such a programme there was significant scope for external actors to provide enlightened support and to inform the domestic processes through making "best practice" developed elsewhere available so that this could be taken into account. The role for the outsider was essentially one of facilitation.

EDI/TI's strategy for anti-corruption work thus relies on facilitating:

- the emergence of a coalition between government and civil society to provide a framework for consultation and support, and to bring civil society (including the private sector) in to the development and implementation of programmes designed to promote, strengthen and protect the country's integrity
- public education through a strengthened media, integrity workshops and increased public voice through service delivery and integrity surveys;
- prevention measures (as more cost-effective and more do-able than enforcement);
  institution building across all sectors (executive, judiciary, media, parliament, private sector, watchdog agencies and civil society); and
- enforcement of the rule of law, and
- an action research (learning by doing) mode where there is a general consensus on the need for action and the political will to do so.

Work in 17 countries (Uganda, Tanzania, Mauritius, Benin, Madagascar, Bolivia, Nicaragua, Jordan, Palestine-Gaza, Ukraine, Georgia, Bulgaria, Bangladesh, Nepal, Pakistan, Latin America, the Middle East, the ex-Soviet bloc and South Africa) will provide important regional examples often more relevant and easier to promote to neighbouring countries. All EDI country-based activities should fit in as part of the Bank's general strategy and the overall larger framework of country assistance strategy (CAS). Collaboration between EDI, Operations, and the Research Team to put the anti-corruption agenda into an effective overall strategy can only facilitate this process of integration.

Where EDI becomes involved, efforts should be tailored carefully to the client's situation. Some approaches based upon the Governance Team's prior experiences have married well into the circumstances of other countries. However, the strategy must at all times remain very adaptable. The model should change as "case law" (or best practice experience) increases with the ultimate objective of improved effectiveness. Surveys can provide evidence of impact and progress made by establishing a baseline from which to judge.

Accepting that there is no blueprint in this area, EDI and its partners work as facilitators in a learning process, piloting SDS in several countries (see Box below). EDI then draws out relevant lessons and disseminates them.

EDI/TI assist governments on how to manage a change process that results in increased transparency and accountability and improved service delivery. These elements create an enabling environment for private sector development and economic growth. One of our strategies is to initiate a process that will force all the stakeholders to make a choice: "either they are part of the problem or they are part of the solution". Increased transparency is developed around:

- the rules of the game, e.g. definition of what constitutes corruption, leadership codes, codes of conduct etc.,
- what services are expected to be delivered by the government; and
- actual corruption cases reported in the media which should make it clear both to the civil servants who have to make choices that would make them corrupt and the integrity pillars outside the government who are supposed to hold the civil service accountable.

One way of measuring the delivery of services is to conduct regular surveys which are costly but useful. These costs, however, could be reduced by decreasing the sample size (for example, for a 50 million person country, a survey of 5,000 might be just as informative as a survey of 50,000). Survey customisation and analysis should contribute toward these ends. It is important to realise that surveys used for pure awareness raising and problem identification will be less involved and smaller than those used for problem description in order to reduce bureaucratic "red tape" and as an input into a broader reform programme. The Service Delivery Surveys (SDS) done in partnership with CIET international fall in the latter category and are deemed to be much more expensive.

A substantial amount of governance work should be completed at the sub-national level. As decentralisation becomes a growing priority, more work still must be done assessing the relative advantages of decentralised analysis and provision of public services. The EDI/TI strategy is to demonstrate an approach which can be incorporated into projects and to act as a resource for NGOs and local institutions in order to eventually hand over the process to the stakeholders and make it " mainstream."

Why Fight Corruption?

Combating corruption, which can be defined as the misuse of public power for private gain, is instrumental to the broader goal of achieving more effective, fair and efficient government. Anti-corruption activists are not only concerned with reducing malfeasance but with mitigating its impact on development and society. Does corruption have a negative impact on alleviating poverty by distorting developmental decision-making? How inefficient is bribery? Who ultimately pays the cost of corruption?

Corruption involves behaviour in which the officials in the public service, whether politicians or civil servants, improperly and unlawfully enrich themselves or those close to them by the misuse of the public power entrusted to them. Corruption may be categorised in at least four different ways:

a) Petty corruption practised by public servants who may be basically decent and honest individuals but who are grossly underpaid, and depend on small bribes from the public to feed and educate their families;
b) Episodic where honest behaviour is the norm, corruption is the exception and the dishonest public servant is disciplined when detected;
c) Systemic where there are strands of corrupt behaviour, trending upwards from the bribe collection points and where the system depends on corruption for its own survival; and
d) Grand corruption of higher public officials and politicians who make decisions involving large public contracts or projects financed by the donor community which is motivated by greed, not need (and may well also be the basis for political party fund-raising by the ruling elite).

It can also be divided into two quite different categories – corruption where benefits flow to the payer of the bribe (bribery); and corruption where payments are extorted from unwilling but resigned clients (extortion). Still others divide corruption into another two categories: bribes to pay for what a person has a legal right to receive; and bribes to pay for benefits to which the payer has no right at all.

A global "typology"?

As the typology of corruption varies from country to country, and because of the number of variables involved, it is unlikely that a detailed attempt to achieve a global, or even regional, "typology" would serve a useful purpose in the field. For example, in some countries the failure to pay a living wage lies, at least in part, at the root of the problem: yet in other countries, well-paid public servants are busying themselves with corruption. In some countries there is the rule of law functioning, and independent judges are ready to review the legality of official actions and provide remedies: in others, the judiciary is suborned, acquiescent or neutralised. Some have law officers who are willing partners in anti-corruption activities, and others have law officers whose legislation and advice seems designed to render corrupters free from the fear of successful prosecution, even if they were detected. In some countries the private sector is well-organised and poised to take on an assertive role; in others, they are weak and not used to having a "voice" or speaking authoritatively to their government.

The actors amenable to the supporting of anti-corruption activities also vary significantly from country to country, thus dictating a careful choice of entry points. Inevitably, this will mean that activities have to be carefully tailored to meet their portfolio responsibilities.

Corruption also flourishes in different fields in different places: land re-zoning, customs, political appointments, income tax, ministerial and other discretions (whose grounds are vague or generalised:

For example, such discretions have been used to exempt personal imports from taxation.

Corruption occurs in all countries, regardless of levels of social economic development. It is most likely to occur where the public and private sector meet, and especially where public officials have a direct responsibility for the provision of public service or the application of specific regulations or levies. For corruption to take place, the following elements must be present: a public official, discretionary power, a misuse of that public power by the public official, a collusion between this official and one or more other officials and a benefit (whether in money and / or in kind) to all the corrupt officials involved.

EDI/TI new approach to governance

Principles and Modus Operandi for EDI/TI's Governance and Anti-Corruption Work

a) EDI/TI work as facilitators focusing on process rather than experts focusing on policy choices. We are also open about the fact that we have more questions than answers and that we would work with our partners in a learning process.

b) EDI/TI only becomes involved on invitation by the government. This is in accordance with the policy articulated by the Bank's President and serves to protect the institution from any suggestion that it is interfering in the internal politics of the client country.

c) There must be a clearly defined government actor responsible and accountable for the programme that is developed and executed. This minimises the possibilities of misunderstandings arising. It also importantly opens the necessary doors for effective work to be undertaken and provides a partner to disseminate what is being accomplished.

d) There must also be a partner in civil society with whom the government is happy to work creatively. This acts as a protection for the institution from its being drawn in to one "side" of a political game and ensures that the work is directed towards getting the system as a whole "right." The involvement of civil society is also essential as governments increasingly appreciate (to a significant extent pioneered and exemplified by the Bank in its own work) that a strong and creative partnership between the government and civil society is central to effective work being undertaken in the integrity area.

e) The process should be one driven by partnership and shared understandings. The internal partnership embraces government, civil society and the Bank. An international NGO as a partner can be a useful lead in civil society. There are a variety of stakeholders in the integrity system, and successful improvement relies on the involvement of as many as possible of these. Having an international NGO as a partner creates avenues into civil society and the contacts leading individuals and opinion makers in the country have with their own government. Such a partnership also helps minimise any risks that there may be for the bank in this admittedly tricky area of activity.

f) Local "ownership" must be achieved quickly and local actors must drive the process; it is naive for outsiders to believe that they can prescribe answers to the domestic corruption problems of other countries. Corruption takes a myriad of forms and the internal dynamics and networks vary subtly but distinctively from country to country. The topic is also extremely sensitive. It is therefore crucial that the process not be driven locally. Locals know their own problems best; they are the best judges of what is possible; and they are the ones who are going to have to bring about the reforms.

g) "Action research" ("learning by doing"): With a shared understanding of objectives among all the partners, and with the process being locally owned and driven, the role of the Bank should be low key and one of helping to identify the questions that should be asked rather than seeking to impose answers to them, and capturing the process (and where possible documenting it) to ensure that lessons learned in one country are available for others (learning by doing). It also creates space for the "exit strategy"; it not only minimises the Bank's temptation to prescribe solutions, but it also makes sense. There are no "off-the- shelf" solutions which the Bank or anyone else can impose or recommend to a country. The Bank's competitive advantage is an ability to ascertain the questions that need to be faced and to feed into the answer-seeking processes whatever external experience is sought by the internal actors.

h) There should be a clear exit strategy. Since governance work is, by definition, never ending, there must therefore be a clear "exit strategy" for EDI/TI, which is also understood by the clients in both government and civil society. The aim should be to focus on relevant "pillars" of the national integrity system to the point where the reform process becomes sustainable and irreversible. A good example of this is the series of investigative journalism training workshops conducted in Uganda and Tanzania. In the course of the initial workshops, local facilitators were trained to the point where they are now able to take over the process and continue it. More than this, in both countries new professional institutions have emerged, part funded by the journalists themselves from their own resources, and in one instance a newspaper, *The Crusader*, has now been established and is regularly on sale in Kampala. Another attempt to create an exit strategy is a Training of Trainers Workshop and took place in August 1997 where EDI's governance team brought all our partners and all our documented experience to 20 senior government officials and 20 key consultants in 8 African countries. The purpose of the meeting was to build a local capacity to improve the government.

New Paradigms driving EDI/TI's Governance and Anti-Corruption Programme

Accountability through transparency

Lack of accountability both for national and international civil servants is probably the most important factor why sustainable development has not taken place in most of the world's poorest countries despite large transfers of money and expertise over the last 30 years. Accountability, integrity and the rule of law are very much dependent on leadership and political will from the top but even with the necessary political will there is no guarantee that there will be the rule of law and sustainable development. In most developing countries less than 2 percent of the population work for government. The EDI/TI governance approach is based on the assumption that accountability can only occur through active education and involvement of the 98 percent of the people outside the government rather than the traditional pressure from the donor community.

The challenge is to look for synergy through sequencing and timing of the two pressure points. Educating and involving the public is the challenge and the centrepiece of the EDI/TI strategy and efforts in these areas are currently being carried out in 6 of our pilot countries. Currently the key elements of the awareness raising and involvement of the public are:

- democratic elections (parliamentary, presidential and local
- increased transparency by opening up the government and by delivering services closer to the customers;
- giving the public an active voice by involving them in periodic service delivery surveys and integrity/corruption surveys; and
- raising public awareness about their rights and responsibilities through public education (strengthening the media and involving them in the "nation building", introducing citizen charters where the public knows what services to expect (quality, cost, timeliness and coverage)

Focus on services to the public

Public Service has forgotten to serve the public and one of the major objectives of EDI RP's governance and anti-corruption work is to facilitate the public service of client countries to improve their service (quality, timeliness, cost and coverage) to their civil society. The Service Delivery Survey (SDS) is an important tool in achieving this objective.

Raise awareness and expectations of the civil society

The rationale for this task can be explained by the example of Mali where a service delivery survey was conducted in 1995. Despite the facts that Mali has some of the worst social indicators in the world the survey indicated that a majority of the population did not have a problem with the current situation. We realised that after so many years of misery they had lost hope and did not expect anything from their government.

Based on this experience the adoption of a "Citizen Charter" model was necessary in addition to periodic service delivery surveys where the client could be assisted in increasing the accountability of the government through:

a) informing the civil society about their rights; what services they are supposed to get from their government, cost, quality and timeliness
b) obtaining more accurate information about the services actually reaching the people at the village level through household service delivery surveys;
c) giving the people a voice, by going back to the people with regular household surveys and initiating a process where this information is returned to: (i) the national and sub-national policy-makers, and (ii) the involved donors in an efficient and effective manner

Strengthen the pillars of integrity

EDIRP Governance and Anti-Corruption Team has, in collaboration with Transparency International (TI), devised the concept of a National Integrity System consisting of 8 "Pillars of Integrity."

The pillars of integrity are:

1) Executive
2) Parliament
3) Judiciary
4) Watchdog Agencies
5) Media
6) Private Sector (Chamber of Commerce, etc.)
7) Civil Society
8) Enforcement Agencies (Police and Prosecution)

EDI's Governance Programme emphasises both the piloting of new approaches to public sector management issues and the dissemination of lessons learned from such pilots and elsewhere.

Our approach involves working with client countries (both government and civil society), international organisations, and donors as partners. Accepting that there is no "blueprint" for enhanced public sector management, the GPSM team works as facilitators in a learning process, rather than as experts with all the answers.

Underlying our general approach are the concepts that there should be, in the public sector: a focus on clients, a results-orientation in the delivery of public services, and enhanced levels of accountability and transparency. As a starting point, we believe that improved governance and public sector management rests on improvements in three areas: strengthened institutional capacity, improved service delivery, and enhanced national integrity.

Reflecting these concepts, the Governance programme comprises three principal activities or changes in mindsets: (i) improving public sector service delivery (results-orientation); (ii) building integrity through promoting accountability and transparency and (iii) capacity building. It dovetails with EDIRP's Public Sector Management Programme which focuses on civil service reform and public expenditure planning and management, as well as one supporting activity research and multi-media dissemination.

Capacity Building and the Involvement of Civil Society in Improving Service Delivery to the Public

In the past most capacity building projects focused on the tools and skills of the government (see Figure 1). Projects would finance infrastructure, computer systems, equipment and conduct all sorts of skills training for technical staff. These activities are important. However, without accountability, transparency and the necessary focus on objectives of the government, the effect of these initiatives are questionable.

The new approach to capacity building encouraged by EDI/TI is introducing two major shifts from the old (see Figure 2):

a) **mindset, integrity and leadership:** In addition to skills and tools focus is also on mindset, integrity and leadership. Mindset refers to the outlook, or state of mind that civil servants are bringing to their jobs. Partners will be encouraged to adopt key changes in mindset relating to: integrity, results-orientation, and the acceptability of civil servants serving the public. Public integrity is defined as: "Honest and open government where policy is made and implemented based on the public good". By leadership EDI/TI will work with its clients to establish standards and ground rules for leaders in the public service by introducing Leadership Codes, Codes of Conducts, Declarations and Monitoring of Assets.

b) **capacity building for all integrity pillars:** The second change is that the audience for the capacity or institution building be broadened to include all the integrity pillars (judiciary, parliament, media, civil society, private sector, enforcement agencies and watchdog agencies. Clients will also be encouraged to strengthen the "integrity pillars" such as the Public Accounts Committee (PAC) in Parliament, Judiciary, Watchdog Agencies, Civil Society pressure groups like local Transparency International chapters and the media to hold senior government officials accountable.

National Integrity Systems

There is considerable evidence that there is strong relationship between the existence and extent of corruption and economic performance. This is giving rise to an increasing demand for good governance, including integrity and transparency, throughout the developing world. Pervasive corruption reduces the efficiency of government in general, and in particular reduces the effectiveness of both provide investment and foreign aid. Transparency helps governments ensure the efficient use of resources.

Corruption also makes citizens feel alienated from their government. In many countries, it is the people themselves who are demanding action to reduce corruption. Leaders in the campaign against corruption can only achieve real gains when a society collectively changes its expectation of public behavior, or when people believe that they are entitled to expect a government that is not corrupt.

In each country where EDI/TI is active, it works in partnership with the government and the civil society to develop a national integrity system consisting of: (a) awareness-raising among the civil society; (b) institution building; (c) prevention of corrupt practices; and (d) prosecution of corrupt officials.

Ultimately, EDI/TI's goal is to empower individuals, communities and governments in client countries with knowledge that enhances their capacity to foster sustainable, equitable development. EDI/TI facilitates seminars for opinion leaders, including parliamentarians, journalists, educators and NGOs, in order to support consensus building and build an informed citizenry. EDI/TI also emphasizes public awareness raising and education through quality programs in the schools and mass media

Building Integrity to Fight Corruption; the Plan for Uganda

The fostering of good governance involves developing a country programme which addresses:

a) Sustainable development
b) Rule of law
c) Enhanced quality of life
d) A re-defined role of the state (creation of an enabling environment for the private sector)

This in turn requires a focus which goes beyond simply providing tools and skill-building and centering activities on central government. This broader focus adds another raft of potential partners in the process. The recognition of the public adds a much broader dimension, both as consumers and as the body to which government is accountable. The strategy therefore must draw on the inputs which can be made by civil society as well, because it emphasizes:

1. increased capacity through changing mindsets and provision of leadership;
2. results-orientation; a focus on clients and client-orientation in the delivery of public services ; and
3. integrity; enhanced levels of accountability and transparency

[1] See, for example, Teaching Note by F. Stapehurst, Good Governance, Private Sector Investment and Economic Growth in Sub-Sahara ; (EDI, forthcoming).

The strategy outline

To reflect the above concepts, the strategy must comprise four principal activities:

a) improving public sector service delivery (SDS);
b) increasing and entrenching levels of accountability and transparency;
c) civil service reform leading to a re-defined role of the state and an enabling environment for private sector development; and
d) public expenditure planning and management based on evidence-based planning involving the civil society in giving a feedback on the government's service delivery.

It is essential for a good governance programme to include the strengthening of national integrity systems and practices. In practical terms this requires that a CAS programme encompass a fully-integrated process in order to consolidate the gains of civil service reform, and to ensure that the success and sustainablility of the reforms has a continuing emphasis on the delivery of services to the public in ways which are not undermined or distorted by corruption.

Important Elements in the Uganda Integrity Strategy

Public Awareness

A major need identified by the consultations leading to the adoption of the Integrity Plan was the raising of public awareness. The levels of corruption which have afflicted Uganda for over a generation have led to public attitudes of acquiescence and acceptance. Although there are increasing examples of members of the public challenging corrupt practices when they encounter them, there is an overwhelming sense of powerlessness among the public, believing that they have no option but to live with corrupt conduct by public officials. This acceptance is made more damaging to the public interest by a tendency to applaud acquisition of wealth which can only have been made corruptly. The needs identified are two: to have the public reject corrupt conduct when they encounter it by reporting it to the appropriate authorities (which must, of course, be those in which they have confidence); and to treat with contempt those in their communities who have acquired wealth illicitly.

"Top Down": The government recognises and accepts that leadership at the highest levels (as, indeed, throughout government institutions and agencies) should be a role-model of conduct of the highest standard. In particular, following upon the holding of free and fair elections, the leadership will have the moral authority to bring to bear on the problem.

To achieve change at the leadership levels, seminars and workshops will be conducted to design appropriate leadership and other codes of conduct and techniques of implementation. In the course of these conferences, leaders will receive the message that corrupt conduct will not be tolerated but will be dealt with firmly and without fear or favour. The same message will be delivered to enforcement agencies, who will be reminded that they are expected to uphold the Rule of Law. Cabinet retreats and seminars for parliamentarians on the subject of integrity were being planned for August 1996.

"Bottom-up": A survey was conducted December 1995 (the focus was service delivery in Health and Agriculture – corruption was perceived by many as a key issue) and another will be conducted (early 1997) with the civil society to find out the perceived extent of corruption in the country. This will establish baselines, based on a survey and inputs from the civil society, against which future progress can be measured (a technique which has been adopted with considerable success in Hong Kong).

The survey will also identify the message that needs to be sent to the public and how this message needs to be sent. At the same time, the involvement of a broad section of the public in the conduct of the survey (both as interviewers and as interviewees) will send a positive message of empowerment to the public at large of itself.

Media Training: To date the government has staged 6 investigative journalism workshops for journalists with facilitation by the EDI. These have been designed to raise levels of skills and of confidence, and have been developed in partnership with (among others) local journalist associations in the mutual recognition that the national interest is served by having a strong, independent and professional media. There is a need for these to continue, by working in particular with the journalists who have performed well in the courses to date, and by further raising their levels of skill and confidence.

There is a need to strengthen and deepen this training, and to include training on investigative journalism for editors and owners of newspapers to encourage the media to take on a "nation-building" role.

Other target groups for awareness raising are:
- lawyers working in the judiciary and or government
- staff responsible for curriculum development in the school system
- religious institutions
- other organisations with a broad interface with civil society

Prevention

A primary focus of the national strategy is on corruption prevention: the cost-effectiveness of prevention over enforcement as a principal approach is self-evident. The national strategy therefore envisages (and it is the government's intention to do so) a focus on overhauling and re-invigorating Standing Orders within the public service. It places primary responsibility on those in management positions for the conduct of their subordinates, and seeks the cooperation of the public service and civil society to identify ways in which existing practices can be modified (and practices changed or abolished) in a simplification of government procedures which should not only render them more effective, fair and transparent but also less amenable to corruption. In this process, particular attention will be paid to public tender procedures so as to ensure that these are open, fair and corruption-free.

Institution building

To accomplish this, the Uganda strategy encompasses a holistic approach in which, working with partners within the country drawn from both government and from civil society, the various institutional "pillars" and practices of a national integrity system are strengthened.

As these "pillars" are inter-dependent and do not stand alone, this involves both catalysing the work of other donors into a coherent framework of reform, identifying gaps and opportunities and embracing such "pillars" as the instruments of accountability and transparency (e.g. parliament, free press, judiciary, Auditor-General, Inspector-General); and the building of public awareness.

Each of the pillars in Uganda's National Integrity System has a vital role to play and requires its own separate attention to its differing needs. These "pillars" include:

1. Parliament (the government is anxious to democratize the operations of the parliament through strengthening the committee system, for example Public Accounts Committee (PAC), in ways to ensure that the parliament can act as an independent check on the executive);

2. The judiciary (work will continue to strengthen and uphold the Rule of Law)
3. Enforcement mechanisms; Prosecution and Police
4. The free press
5. Civil society (the government is determined to foster an enabling environment for a vibrant civil society and, in particular, to work with appropriate NGOs such as Transparency Uganda), and
6. Government accountability mechanisms (including the office of the Auditor-General).
7. Inspector General of Government (IGG). In the new Constitution IGG is reporting to Parliament instead of the President.

Private Sector; while the government's role is to stop civil servants from demanding and taking bribes, the private sector should try to stop the civil society from offering bribes ("speed-money", influence peddling)

Enforcement

The national strategy system will be fatally flawed if it fails to fairly but firmly discipline those who transgress the rules. Therefore, while the reforms should be spearheaded by prevention (including the raising of public awareness), at the same time attention is needed to ensure that enforcement agencies are enabled to operate independently and professionally.

Since fighting or curbing corruption is a new field, where little progress has been made in the developing world so far, there is a strong need to try out new approaches. The EDI Governance unit has for this reason initiated an Action Research Approach where we are admitting that we are involved in a learning process where we are willing to try out lots of new approaches in partnership with our clients. The impact of these new approaches, tried out in 15 different client countries, are however monitored carefully through the following short, medium and long-term impact assessment tools (see Figure 2)

To meet the challenges of building up a sustainable national integrity system, firm principles need to be applied. First, the effort must be wholly Ugandan-owned and driven. In particular, the President will have a central role to play in setting the tone and asserting his undoubted moral authority. Second, there is a need to draw civil society in to the process in imaginative and constructive ways. By involving civil society we will do more than capitalise on what it has to offer: it will also generate public confidence in the determination of the undertaking. Third, expectations will need to be managed carefully, to ensure that promises are not unrealistic, that the public starts to see (and continues to see) change on the ground. Fourth, a high level of co-ordination within the government will be needed, as the various actors and stakeholders execute the action programme. Successes and progress will need to be shared, and activities monitored to strict timetables. At the same time, developments will need to be communicated to the public to maintain its confidence in the process. Finally, the donors too will need to co-ordinate amongst themselves (including NGOs as well as donor governments). The undertaking will be altogether too all-embracing to allow for the luxury of ad hoc assistance.

The process will need to be event-driven. The annual national integrity workshop is expected to produce an action plan with a timetable, with benchmarks and staggered events, and monitoring tools put in place as soon as possible. The use of public opinion surveys, which proved so successful in the Hong Kong reform efforts, should be a feature—and these should focus on both levels of corruption and levels of service provided to the public. The action plan calls for major initiatives in four separate areas: i) awareness raising (both top down and bottom up); ii) institution building; iii) prevention (by minimising opportunities and increasing risks of detection); and iv) enforcement.

This can be done through a series of workshops oriented towards the preparation and periodic revision of action plans (assigning responsibilities and setting time-tables) coupled with regular monitoring of progress as a principle tool in the reform process. These should not be thought of as information sharing or awareness raising or any other traditional forms of workshop which have hitherto been held in Uganda. Rather they should be regarded as action-oriented and impact focused. The results of the monitoring will be disseminated widely to keep the public informed of progress and to invite the participation of civil society as a constructive but independent and critical partner.

All of these actions, and others not mentioned, will inevitably require elements of donor funding. For the programme to proceed in a coherent way, there would be considerable advantages in having a group of donors collectively support our efforts in this area.

Partners in the processes

As the Uganda National Strategy was developed by the government in cooperation with civil society, so too is its implementation process that must draw from a wide range of inputs, both from within government and from civil society.

Indeed, one of the beliefs that has guided the deliberations to date has been the conviction that participation by civil society - and the engendering of confidence among the public that the government is serious about the problem of corruption - is fundamental to the attainment of our shared objectives.

Some lessons from the past

Several key elements have been identified that can block progress:

Limits of power exist at the top. An in-coming administration may wish to tackle corruption but inherits a corrupt bureaucracy that impedes efforts to change or is in the grip of traditional party interests able to effectively circumscribe an administration's room for manoeuvre.

A lack of commitment and leadership. Overlay ambitious promises have led to unrealistic and unachievable expectations and a consequent loss of public confidence. Unrealistic and unachievable programmes are frequently the product of corrupt administrations who seek a fig-leaf but resist fundamental change.

Reforms have been piece-meal and uncoordinated. No one has "owned" the reforms. No politician or group within civil society has been fully committed to the reform strategy, striven to implement it and monitored its progress. There has been no "champion".

Reforms have relied too much upon legal remedies. The law is an uncertain instrument with which to attempt to change human behavior. Too much reliance on enforcement can lead to repression, apparent abuse of the power of enforcement and the emergence of yet further corruption.

Enforcement has "overlooked" those at the top and focused only on the "small fry". The law, if applied unfairly and unevenly, soon ceases to be applied at all. It certainly loses its legitimacy and becomes instead a weapon of oppression.

Reforms have lacked a specific focus. In failing to deliver any "quick wins", reforms have soon lost public support. Even when reforms have been focused and changes real, they have not endured where institutional mechanisms do not outlive their leaders.

Corruption is perceived to yield high profits at low risk. The inability or reluctance of the government to prosecute any top level corruption suspects and to imprison them if found guilty have left the public cynical and the culprits confident that corruption is a "low-risk and high-profit" activity. It has fed perceptions that either the elite are all in it together, or that the corrupt who have been caught out "know where the bodies are buried" and would be able to point their fingers at other members of the elite were they to be taken to court. The target of any corruption reform effort must be to render corruption "high risk and low profit".

Reforms that work in one country may not work in another. Approaches to containing corruption, such as the Leadership Codes in Africa, have been abysmal failures, yet the same approach for many years worked well in Papua New Guinea. Similarly, attempts to translate the Hong Kong ICAC approach into an African setting have been dismal failures (although it is too early to judge the initiative in Botswana).

Solo attempts by the government alone. Unilateral attempts by the government to achieve change without the participation of civil society and the private sector has invariably met with minimal successes, save in their most exceptional of circumstances (e.g. Singapore, Hong Kong). Importance of involving the top (president as "champion")

Mainstreaming the lessons learned

EDI builds sustainability by disseminating best practice to improve local capacity and promote partnership. The list of partnerships who are expected to continue the work done after EDI exits include Transparency International, CIET international, Municipal Development Programme (MODP) in Zimbabwe, Canadian Parliamentary Centre, International Centre for Policy Studies (Ukraine), Corporacin Latinoamerica para el Desarrollo (Latin America), Afro-Aid (Tanzania), and WANAD (West Africa). Intellectual partnership is currently being pursued with the OECD, UNDP, IMF, Transparency International, universities, and other consultants. Part of this partnership in 1997 has included participation in international conferences such as the International Anti-Corruption Conference in Lima, the IMF International Conference on Corruption in Lisbon, and the OECD-UNDP Conference on Good Governance in Paris.

It is this replicability and ability to be disseminated which contributes to 'mainstreaming' awareness and prevention activities. For example, in the survey done in Ukraine, the households survey was conducted by the EDI in collaboration with PSD group of the Bank based closely upon modalities developed by CIETinternational. Afro-Aid has also been doing surveys based upon these approaches. USAID has started national integrity workshops in a number of countries. Bolivia already conducted a 'National Integrity Workshop' (called the National Dialogue) and a number of activities before starting their partnership with EDI. In Tanzania and Uganda, a number of local initiatives such as local integrity workshops, municipal awareness -raising activities have been created and implemented. These examples suggest that the experience gained by EDI during its action research is able to be disseminated and is replicable. EDI then keeps its niche because it is constantly innovating. Again, in the case of Bolivia, EDI listened to the needs of the Bolivian government and created new instruments and new ideas to help them with their programme. In this way, as the EDI strategy is incorporated into projects and acts as a resource for NGOs and local institutions, stakeholders eventually take over and the process is 'mainstreamed'

Index

Accountability 5, 38–49, 58, 127, 166
Action Research 160, 165, 174, 178
Against Corruption 6, 7, 14, 25–49, 69, 144
America 23, 51, 160, 177
Annual Evaluation Boards 95
Auditor General 14, 17, 27, 30, 49, 58, 94, 96, 173
Canadian Parliamentary Centre 177
Central Authority Section 116
Central government 93, 98, 99, 100, 101, 102, 170
Central Tender Board 63, 66, 95
China 89, 142
Church Missionary Society 131
Citizen Charter 167
Civil Service 1, 11, 12, 26, 39, 40, 42, 44, 49, 50, 71, 92, 97,
Civil Service Reform programme 97
Commission 5, 14, 15, 17, 19, 32, 36, 38, 39, 42, 52, 53, 72, 89, 94, 95, 129, 138, 142, 144, 146
Constitution 7, 28, 39, 43, 39, 41, 46, 58, 82, 85, 86, 95, 97, 109, 111, 117, 127, 138, 174
Corruption 111, 114, 121, 128, 129, 130, 141, 143, 144, 146, 160, 166, 169, 171, 172, 173, 174, 175, 176, 177
Crime 25, 29, 30, 31, 34, 36, 54, 53, 109, 110, 111, 113, 114, 115, 117, 119, 121, 122, 123, 125, 126, 127, 128, 129
Criminal Investigation Department 29, 110, 121
Criminal law 115, 128
DANIDA 146
Decentralisation 2, 32, 92–105, 161
Decentralisation Statute 102
Democratic elections 166
Director of Public Prosecutions 2, 28, 109, 129
District associations 102
District local council chairpersons 98
District Petition Committees 35, 36
District Service Committees 94
Economic Development 5, 38, 55, 108, 143, 159, 163
EDIRP Governance and Anti-Corruption Team 167
Education 2, 15, 19, 32, 72, 74, 80, 82, 84, 85, 88, 97, 106, 130, 136, 160, 166, 170
Electoral practices 98
Equalisation Grants 104
European Commission 38
Evidence 51, 129
Executive 15, 22, 35, 83, 90, 94, 160, 168, 173
Extortion 48, 53, 79, 85, 162
Fingerprint Bureau 122
Force Dog Section 123
Fraud Section 114
Freedom of Information Act 157
Governance Team 160
Governance team 165
Government, Local Statute 97
GPSM 168
Grade III Magistrates Courts 118
Grand corruption 162
Grand corruption 46, 47, 48, 49, 144
ICAC 177
Identification Bureau 122, 124
IMF 177
Information laws 13

Inspector General of Government (IGG) 4, 28, 38, 56, 71, 75, 77, 94
Inspectorate and Research Division 111, 112
Institution Building 14
Institution building 6, 173, 10, 160, 169, 170, 175
Integrity 1, 4, 5, 6, 7, 97, 99, 101, 103, 105, 107, 159, 161,
Inter-district co-operation 102
International Anti-Corruption 177
International Centre for Policy Studies (Ukraine) 177
Interpol 125
Investigative journalism training 144, 165
Investigative journalists 3, 143, 158
Italian 51
Journalists 2, 3, 7, 73, 131–135, 137, 138, 140, 141, 143–148, 155, 156, 158, 165, 170, 172
Judiciary 7, 15, 29, 30, 40, 44, 45, 109, 110. 112, 126, 159, 160, 163, 168, 169, 173, 174
Lay prosecutors 112, 117, 118
Leadership Codes 58, 161, 169, 177
Living wage 11, 42, 71, 163
Local 20, 91, 93, 94, 95, 97, 98, 105, 121, 165
Local Governance 98
Management systems 14, 101, 110, 114
Media 3-7, 13, 25, 68,70, 71, 73, 74, 95, 99, 108, 135, 137, 131–147, 150–152, 154, 156, 160, 161, 166, 168, 169, 170, 172
Mengo Court 131, 117, 118
Ministry of Finance 63, 64, 93
Ministry of Internal Affairs 124
Ministry of Justice and Constitutional Affairs 116
Mukono National Integrity Workshop 6
Municipal Development Programme 177
National Integrity Committee 1
National Integrity System 1, 4, 5, 7, 105–107, 165, 167, 170, 173, 174
National Resistance Council 33, 34
Newspaper editors 73, 155
NRM government 4, 20, 28, 58, 76, 120, 124, 141
OECD 177
OECD-UNDP Conference on Good Governance in Paris 177
Parliament 30, 41, 57, 58, 78, 83, 86, 90, 137, 168, 169, 173, 174, 177
Police Act 28, 129
Police force 29, 34, 111, 119, 120, 121, 123, 124, 125
Poverty 8, 24, 72, 82, 98, 100, 127, 159, 162
Presidential Commission 144
Press 40, 44, 106, 127, 132, 135, 138
Prevention of Corruption Act of 1970 6, 128
Private Eye 151
Private Sector 8–12, 15, 25, 45, 48, 74, 81, 97, 168, 170, 174
Privatisation 11, 39, 40, 45, 49, 72, 103, 107
Procurement 2, 11, 14, 15, 20, 45, 48
Prosecution 12, 15, 31, 36, 37, 57, 83, 86, 110, 111, 112, 113, 114, 115, 116, 117, 119, 121, 122, 126, 163, 168, 170, 174
Public Accounts Committee 1, 15, 20, 30, 34, 58, 94, 169
Public Prosecutions 2, 28, 109,

Public Sector Review Commission 42
Public Service 2, 5, 17, 19, 23, 26, 32, 33, 62, 76, 94, 167
Religious institutions 6, 106, 173
Research 61, 111, 112, 113, 118, 148, 155, 160, 165, 168, 174, 178
Resident State Attorneys 112, 117, 118, 126
Results-orientation 1, 97
Senior civil servants 43, 39, 40
Service delivery 97, 105, 140, 159, 160, 161, 166, 167, 168, 171, 172
Standing Orders 42, 173
The Citizen 148, 149, 157
The Crusader 141
The Exposure 149
The Penal Code (Amendment) Statute 1987 27
The Prevention of Corruption Act 1970 27, 45
The Public Finance Act 28
The Secrets Act 132, 152, 157
Transparency 2, 5, 7, 38, 39, 41, 43, 45, 47, 49, 51, 89, 107, 108, 143,146, 159, 167, 169, 174, 177
UNDP 177
UNESCO 140
WANAD (West Africa) 177
World Bank 5, 7, 42, 51, 64, 65, 143, 159